America in Cross-Stitch

Other books by Ann Roth:

Jerusalem in Needlepoint and Embroidery
Mosaics of the Holy Land
Mosaics of Ravenna

America in Cross-Stitch

Designs by Ann Roth

TWENTY AMERICAN LANDSCAPES AND LANDMARKS WITH DESCRIPTIONS
AND DETAILED INSTRUCTIONS FOR CROSS-STITCHING

PRENTICE-HALL, INC., Englewood Cliffs, N.J.

All rights reserved

No part of this publication may be reprinted

without the prior permission of the publishers.

First American edition published by Prentice-Hall Inc., 1976.

© 1976 by Massada Press Ltd., Jerusalem

Library of Congress catalogue card number: 76-27326

ISBN 0-13-024125-3

Produced by TAL INTERNATIONAL, Givatayim

PRINTED IN ISRAEL

by Peli Printing Works Ltd.

Table of Contents

ACKNOWLEDGEMENT

*The Publisher would like to thank the following people for assistance in the
preparation of this book:*

*Wallis Mayers and Anne Cheek Landsman for the "Instructions and Uses"
sections. (The kind assistance of the DMC Corporation, Paternayan Bros.,
Inc., the Spinnerin Yarn Co., Joan Toggit, Ltd., and the Counted Thread
Society of America is also gratefully acknowledged.)*

*For the design texts: Patricia Penton Leimbach, Phyllis Hughes, Walker A.
Tompkins, Barbara Creter, Maureen Doyle, Mary Kennan, Eileen Nash,
Tom Miller, Patricia Reinhardt, Kyle W. Riseley, and Claudia Sammartino.*

Preface

When I was asked to make an embroidery book on America, I was delighted and frightened at the same time. Delighted because it would give me the opportunity to cross the ocean and visit a country—although thousands of miles away—so close to Europe in culture, history, and language. Frightened because I knew America was a huge and varied land. How could I make a choice of only twenty scenes for a book?

For ten years I had specialized in cross-stitching buildings and scenery; at first the subjects were only Dutch ones, later I made a book on Jerusalem. From the beginning it was clear to me that it was necessary to see a subject myself, before I could make a design of it. Working from pictures or photographs is impossible, because of the differences in color between the real thing and its picture. So now I would have to go to America to look at it with cross-stitch eyes! The many European countries I had visited offered so many monuments and historical buildings, that in my mind America, being so large, would offer thousands of possibilities. In total I spent nine weeks in the United States, partly by car, partly in a coast-to-coast bus tour. (Although travelling by car is much more interesting, it would certainly have taken twice as much time had I journeyed only that way.) Apart from the countryside I visited most of the big cities, a number of state capitals, "open-air museums," and national parks. Besides the guided tours which were included in the trip, I often hired a cab for one or more hours, sitting in the front next to the driver. In every city or town, cab drivers know exactly where to go. They can show you not only the tourist places, but also the "local color" of their area. Talking to the driver about the population, habits, way of living, etc., was perhaps one of the most interesting parts of my stay. Apart from the included trips, I tried to find others organized specially for Americans, or suggested by American friends, to learn not only the interesting things for people from abroad, but what seemed to interest Americans themselves. In spite of all this it must be clear that after all I saw just a tiny bit of your country, out of which I chose the twenty subjects included herein.

To enable myself to make a choice my "working plan" was built up out of three categories: nature; historic buildings or scenes; and cities, towns, and "living surroundings."

Nature in America is breathtaking. The creative power of the Colorado River—with the help of the seasons—has forced the earth to show all its beauty of form and color. To me Grand Canyon was very beautiful, Bryce Canyon incredible. I never saw such beauty before, nor do I believe I could see it anywhere else. But translating this into cross-stitch—although tempting—was impossible (at least within the time schedule for the book). The same is true for the "Natural Wonders" of Yosemite Park and other places. After all, cross-stitch has its limits, and so have I. Fortunately the Rocky Mountains and the cactus flowers covering the open desert gave me the opportunity to make at least two designs in pure nature.

Finding historic places, scenes, or buildings is a totally different story. As your history started at the eastern and western coasts, the coastal states are the best places to find historic remnants. But what does one do with the hundreds of signs, telling you to enter a lane, at the end of which is found just a dated memory-plate, interesting perhaps for history-minded people, but not for my purpose. Moreover, many historic buildings have been lost in your admirable, but sometimes destructive striving for growth. I am told that in the last ten years a movement is underway to save what is left, resulting in open-air museums. Many of these are in New England, and I visited most of them. I finally chose Port Mystic because it seemed the most scenic one. My final choice was partly made because of the importance of a particular building (i.e. Old State House in Boston, Independence Hall, Philadelphia), and partly because it would make a nice picture (as Carmel Mission does).

The last category—cities, towns, and villages—was a rather difficult one. Although I found exceptions, mostly in New England, I was astonished to see the spoiled skylines and city centers in so many places I visited. It made me think of an unplanned garden, where beautifully flowering violets are no longer visible, because someone (without asking!) thought it better to plant bushes about, while a third person planted trees in between. From the cities I have seen I liked New York, Washington, San Francisco, and New Orleans best. In a way the contrast between the Old State House and the surrounding skyscrapers in Boston has some charm, but it makes your first State House look so little.

The first state capital I visited was Atlanta, and I was thrilled at the view of the golden dome, shining in the modern skyline. I immediately thought: this is special—I will make this! Then I saw Denver and Dallas and other cities, and found they all looked somewhat the same. How to make clear that Atlanta was meant? This difficulty is certainly due to the fact that I look at your country with European eyes. In Europe, Paris, London, and Amsterdam can by no means be mistaken for each other. So I gave up my idea of embroidering a state capitol. Then when I entered by car from Canada into Michigan, I saw the red barns, and thought: this is special, this is Michigan. Afterward I saw them back in Pennsylvania and Vermont, and realized that no one would know I had meant Michigan. Which brings me to perhaps the most striking thing, to me, about America: "nature" aside, passing a state border does not make any difference in the man-made scenery. Farms, churches, houses, and skylines will remain the same, all the streets and roads will be straight, with few windings, cosy corners, or squares. (Moreover, all over you will find the same kinds of buildings selling the same hot dogs, burgers, and drinks.) Of course, I could sometimes find a "local color" in places like California and New Orleans, but even there you find the tendency of being alike. In my opinion it makes America strong and weak at the same time. In a way it was easy to make a choice of twenty striking designs; in a way I could have done a hundred!

But in making a choice one thing is the most important of all: the finished embroideries should be attractive enough for you to want them in your home.

May 1976

CROSS-STITCH MAP OF THE U.S.A.

What better way to start a book called *America in Cross-Stitch* than with America in cross-stitch? A cross-stitch map of the U.S. can make a handsome addition to your home (instructions for adding Alaska and Hawaii can be found on page 90). You can color your map by regions (Southeast, Northwest, Midwest, etc.); by directions (North, South, East, West); by state nicknames (California—Golden State, Florida—Sunshine State, etc.); by state flowers (Illinois—violet, Alabama—camellia); by historical breakdown (13 Original Colonies, Louisiana Purchase, etc.)—or simply according to your own special "association colors" for each state. (The map pictured is embroidered in the colors Ann Roth chose to "tell something" about each state.)

A cross-stitch map could be a useful tool for a child's education, or a picture for his or her room. Travel-minded adults won't mind having one about, either.

Diagram page 90

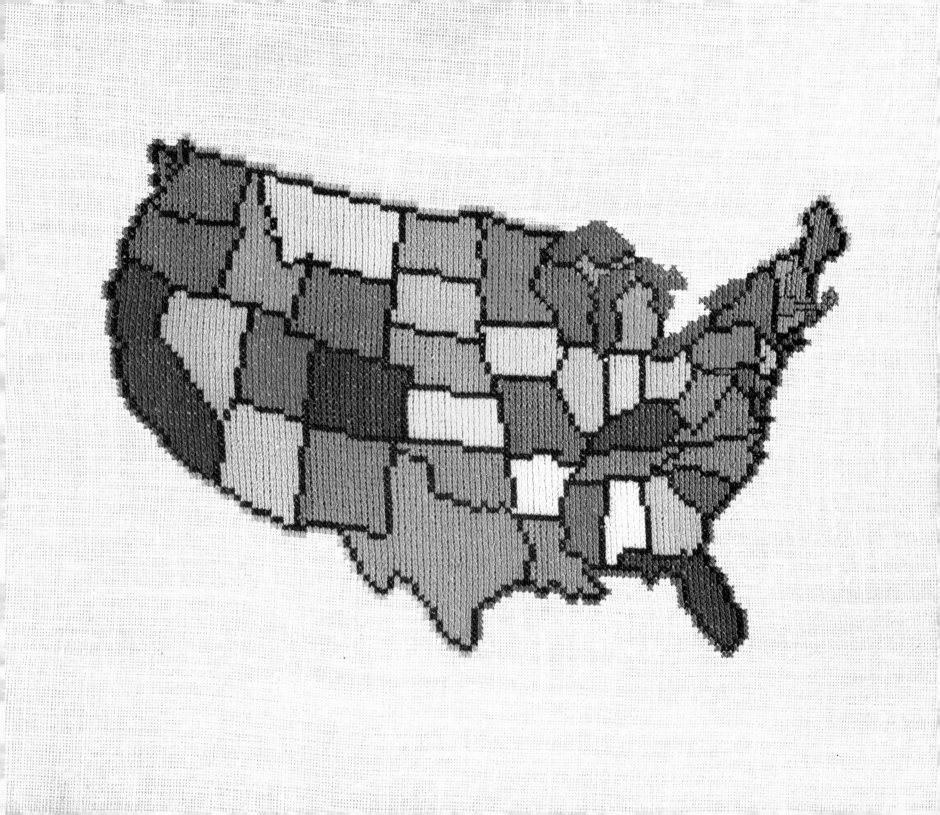

EVERYVILLAGE, VERMONT :: *Second Chance at Eden*

A small portion of every American's heart goes "home" to a village in Vermont—no particular village, but an "everyvillage" nestled in a valley between white birch and pine-covered hills.

It has a neat town square with a Revolutionary War monument, faced about with town hall, Congregational Church, public library, and general store. Somewhere around the village a rambling inn speaks of "summer people" and "winter people," moneyed people from Boston and New York, borrowed elegance and staid gentility, a noble age of class and programmed leisure. On the outskirts of town stately buildings and spacious lawns say prep school, academy, seminary, college. The whole setting is done in white clapboard laced together with maple trees hung with sap buckets in season. There's a veiled illusion that a horse-drawn buggy (or in winter a sledge) belongs to this setting of peace and contentment. A God's-eye view above and beyond Everyvillage, Vermont, catches hints of bucolic pastures, of silos and red barns. Down from the hills through the pine forest, across the meadows, a brook cuts a stoney path to a millrace that runs beneath a covered bridge.

Whence cometh this mythical Eden? It's a composite dream from myriad sources —"The Devil and Daniel Webster," Robert Frost, travel posters, ski brochures, maple syrup labels, college catalogues, and *Yankee* magazine. It embodies the ideals of an *Our Town* and obscures the realities of a *Peyton Place*. But for the most part the dream exists because Vermont exists nearly as beautiful in the twentieth century as in the eighteenth. For all its freeways sheared through granite outcrops and its many swinging ski resorts, Vermont retains its integrity. Its stubborn citizens still troop to town meetings to protest the trappings of "over-civilization." Zoning committees and historical societies cling jealously to the Early American heritage.

Though the dream pretends that milk and maple syrup and water-driven mills are still the economic lifeblood of the state, reality acknowledges that Vermont is a rural retreat where everyone owes much to the tourist trade. Arts and crafts abound. Music and drama flourish in workshops and colleges. Prowling about the commons of a Vermont village you will meet transplants from New Jersey, New York, Rhode Island, from Boston, New Haven, and Baltimore—all assuming proprietary airs about the Green Mountain State. But you may well seek through the other forty-nine without finding a single Vermonter. Given a second crack at Eden, it seems, nobody chooses to leave.

Diagram page 91

A HARBOR VIEW OF PORTSMOUTH, NEW HAMPSHIRE

The tapestry that is Portsmouth begins early in our nation's history. Oldest community in New Hampshire, the city was settled c. 1623. Up until the Revolution, it was the colony's capital. Blessed with a good harbor, at the mouth of the Piscataqua River, Portsmouth reflects the variety of trades bequeathed by the sea. Prosperous merchants built handsome Georgian and Federal-style homes that can be viewed today in an enduring harbor vista. Shipbuilding, lumbering, fishing, and whaling added wealth, bustle, and flavor to this busy port. And across the river, the Portsmouth U.S. Naval Base and Shipyard to this day is a center of seagoing activity—but now you'll see submarines putting in for repair rather than four-masters. Clean white pine masts and spars carved from White Mountain forests were a profitable export from Colonial Portsmouth, N.H., to Portsmouth, England. And good New England timber was put to use in Portsmouth, N.H., shipyards to build privateers and men-of-war during the American Revolution and the War of 1812. Today the exports are shoes, cable, wire, and electric products. Scan the harbor and you'll see the prominent steeple of St. John's Episcopal Church, built in 1807. Inside is a pipe organ dating from 1708, possibly the oldest in the United States. On a stroll through Portsmouth, you'll see the strawberry symbol—on signs that identify a walking tour of the Strawbery Banke restoration. This encompasses a ten-acre site of the original Portsmouth settlement, and includes thirty or more buildings near the harbor that date from the late 1600s to the early 1800s. "The handsomest house in Portsmouth," said George Washington of the Governor Langdon home on Pleasant Street. John Langdon served as Governor of New Hampshire five times, and was the first *pro tempore* President of the U.S. Senate. His house, built in 1784, is one of many fine homes of the Colonial period now open to the public, offering the traveller a fine view of typical residences of New England citizens of note: General William Whipple, a signer of the Declaration of Independence; John Paul Jones (his ship *Ranger* was built in a nearby shipyard); Daniel Webster (his house is part of the Strawbery Banke restoration); Thomas Bailey Aldrich, noted author and editor. The Jackson House (c. 1664) provides a well-preserved example of our early Colonial heritage, a glimpse into the seventeenth century. The Warner House (1716) is a splendid example of Georgian architecture, one of the handsomest in New England. Another lovely Georgian structure is the Wentworth Gardner House (1760). The merchants of Portsmouth built well.

Tourism is a key industry in the New Hampshire of today. Although the coast of New Hampshire is only 18 miles long, it is a very popular resort area and Portsmouth is the focus of hurried summer migrations. A quiet view of Portsmouth harbor offers a pleasant change of pace, for here is an authentic and delightful reflection of early America.

Diagram page 92

MYSTIC SEAPORT, CONNECTICUT

You are back in the age of sail: tall-masted ships dot the harbor; nineteenth-century homes line the cobblestone road leading to the wharves; the ship carver's shop, ropewalk, ship chandlery, and apothecary all invite you to relive an important period in America's past. This is Mystic Seaport, Connecticut. Although only a short distance from New York City, this town is over one hundred years apart in time. Its roads, buildings, stores, and especially its sail-filled harbor attest that you are back in the 1800's, in a village that grew and flourished from shipbuilding and the sea. Thanks to the foresight and determination of three men, Carl C. Cutler, Edward E. Bradley, and Dr. Charles K. Stillman, Mystic Seaport lives today, recreating for future generations the industry and lifestyles of America's maritime era. These three men founded the Maritime Historical Society in 1929, which today operates and maintains a number of maritime museums, period homes, and shops boasting the craftsmanship of nineteenth-century New England.

Mystic Seaport is the only museum of its kind. Over 150 sailing vessels have been refurbished and set afloat in its harbor. Visitors are welcome to board several of these ships to view the crew's quarters and equipment outfitting the sailors on their fishing, trading, and whaling expeditions. One of these, the *Charles W. Morgan*, is the last wooden whaleship in existence. Over one-half million persons explore its decks annually. Its history, voyages, ports of call, owners, cargoes, outfittings, and repairs are all carefully documented. Original entries in the ship's logs and journals throw much light on both the hazards and profits of America's whaling industry.

During its peak of activity, around 1851, Mystic Seaport's 14 working shipyards supplied sturdy vessels for journeys to the West Indies, Europe, the Far East, and California via Cape Horn. Today the same stores that outfitted sailors over one hundred years ago are still hard at work. Visitors to Mystic Seaport can view restored, ornate figureheads in the ship carver's shop. The town's ropewalk offers demonstrations of the rope-making process so vital to the shipping industry. And the ship chandlery is open daily, tempting bypassers with its supplies of salted meats, tobacco, and rum, as well as the lanterns, anchors, boots, and oilskins that every ship's "husband" or supply officer stocked prior to setting sail.

Beneath Mystic Seaport's calm, mid-nineteenth-century exterior, the activities of restoration and conservation are constantly under way. Expert craftsmen check wooden artifacts for decay and termites. Iron pieces are chemically treated to preserve their form and function. A crew of repairmen work daily renovating the roofs, masts, and rigging of Mystic Seaport's impressive fleet. Sails are cleaned; wooden replacement pieces are hand-carved in the tradition of craftsmanship that made Mystic Seaport a thriving shipbuilding center.

But all this work is worthwhile, as any visitor to Mystic Seaport will confirm.

Diagram page 93

THE OLD BOSTON STATE HOUSE

Few American cities can boast the historical heritage of Boston, and fewer yet landmarks could claim more action seen than Boston's Old State House. Featured on the "Freedom Trail," it has over the years been referred to as "The Town House in Boston," "Court House in Boston," "The Province Court House," "The State House," and "The City Hall." Its history explains how it earned these various titles.

The earliest recorded use of this site dates to a Puritan marketplace—including a pillory and stocks—as early as 1634. For almost a century this spot on what was then called King Street served as a "civic pivot point." In 1657 (partly because a philanthropic gentleman living nearby took pity on the people gathering in the rain) a multipurpose "Town House" was erected. A European-style wooden building with open sides, it contained not only the Council of the Royal Governors, Representatives Hall, Deputies of the General Court, the Judiciary, and rooms for town officials, but also a small town library. In the heart of Boston's bustling market area, the square out front of the Town House became a public meeting place, and the site of much political protest and demonstration. In 1711 the Town House was completely destroyed by fire. A larger building—called the State House—was constructed on the same plot of land, but it, too, was gutted by fire, leaving only walls. Invaluable records, furniture, and royal portraits all perished. Since many of the destroyed items were irreplaceable, plans were made for a second building in another part of the city—Faneuil Hall—to share the record-keeping functions of the State House.

In the State House as it stands today, pirates including Captain Kidd stood before Lord Governor Bellomont to be tried. The gallery set up in Representatives Hall in 1763 was the first public visitors' gallery (in a legislative body) in the Western World. The square out front of the State House was the scene of the infamous Boston massacre, when on March 5, 1770, British soldiers led by Captain Preston encountered a rowdy protest group nicknamed "The Bully Boys." Preston and his men were tried in the Council Chamber of the State House the following October. James Otis read his famous tirade against the Writs of Assistance in the State House. And on July 18, 1776, the Declaration of Independence was publicly read for the first time on the balcony facing King St. (now State St.). That evening all royal emblems were removed and burned. In 1789, when a victorious George Washington visited Boston, a special review balcony was built in his honor. In 1834 William Lloyd Garrison sought refuge from lynchers in the State House. And by 1865, the building was no longer the "City Hall" but a business center, for a new city hall had been located on School St. By this time, the building was badly in need of renovation. When town officials hesitated to approve the necessary repairs and considered tearing the building down, their decision to appropriate the necessary funds was cinched when the city of Chicago bid to move the landmark to a new home, rather than allow its destruction.

Presently the building is maintained by The Bostonian Society as a museum containing many priceless portraits, prints, samples of Colonial clothing, and a fine collection from America's maritime past. The outside decor includes the majestic lion and unicorn, famed symbols of the British Crown, restored in 1880. A gentle anachronism amid the skyscrapers of Modern America, the Old State House is a striking reminder of the steps to freedom.

Diagram page 94

MOUNT VERNON ⠒ *Washington's Home*

When George Washington inherited Mount Vernon from his older half-brother, it was already a large estate. To it he added lands from Martha B. Custis' dowry, plus another 2,000 acres, for a total of 10,000 acres. On this land he first grew tobacco, and then switched to wheat, rye, corn, and flax. During the Revolutionary War and his two terms in the Presidency, Washington entrusted the various parts of the land to several overseers and gardeners. But when he was at home, Washington lived the disciplined life of a gentleman farmer.

He generally rose at five to read and write. After breakfast at seven, he rode out to check the progress of his crops, the condition of the buildings, and to consult with the overseers. Aside from the cultivated fields, Washington also kept formal gardens which impressed his European guests. For a meat supply, Washington kept sheep, pigs, and deer. He also seined the Potomac for shad and haddock, catching enough to be able to sell them by the thousands. To prepare his grain for consumption, Washington kept a mill and a distillery. He sold most of the whiskey from the distillery, and used the mash to feed his pigs.

Washington's ordered life did not lead him to neglect his guests, however. At two each afternoon he returned for dinner, an elegant affair often served on Sèvres porcelain. Afterwards he would entertain his guests with tours of the property, riding, and conversation. Tea at seven was followed by more conversation. At nine the general retired for the night.

Washington was childless, and perhaps this is why he lavished so much attention on Mount Vernon. After his death, the estate passed to his nephew, Bushrod Washington. The estate was kept in the family until 1853, when John Augustine Washington, Jr., decided to sell the estate to the national government or to the State of Virginia. The buildings were by then in a state of great disrepair, and the governments were not interested. In 1853, Ann Pamela Cunningham first heard of the conditions at Mount Vernon. Sightseers were taking souvenir chips from Washington's grave, and had removed most of the original furniture from the house. Miss Cunningham formed the Mount Vernon Ladies' Association to purchase Mount Vernon and restore it.

Today the results of their work can be seen in the mansion and the many other original and reconstructed buildings. Repaired and refurbished, with gardens recreated and much of the furniture restored, the old plantation brings to life the atmosphere which nourished the economic and social life of the eighteenth-century South. Sixteen miles below Washington, D.C., on the south bank of the Potomac, the spirit of George Washington, statesman, military strategist, gentleman and agriculturist, survives.

This view is the famous "West Front," of which an original sketch exists in Washington's own hand.

Diagram page 95

INDEGENDENCE HALL ⠆ *Philadelphian Gem*

Pennsylvania was founded by William Penn as a sanctuary for Quakers, but the freedom of thought it extended to all men quickly attracted all manner of freethinkers. Philadelphia, chief city of the colony, grew prosperous as the principal market for the products of the Delaware watershed. This prosperity and the diverse and fast-growing population combined to make Philadelphia a center of art, politics, and fashion. It became the unofficial headquarters for the American Revolution, and from 1790 to 1800, it was the Federal capital.

Independence Hall, originally the Pennsylvania State House, was built in the midst of this intellectual, political, and mercantile ferment. It was designed about 1730 by Andrew Hamilton, former governor of the colony, and Edmund Wooly, master carpenter. Both were members of the Carpenters' Company which was responsible for the buildings adjacent to the site. Together with the completed Hall (for a while called Carpenters' Hall) these became the first civic center in America.

Completed in 1748, Independence Hall is an example of the modest scale of Georgian buildings, which once lent Philadelphia much of its "character." A two-story brick building, it is as tall as most domestic housing of the era. However, it is distinguished by a length of 100 feet, and by marble panels in the facade, a typical architectural device of Georgian public buildings. The wooden tower and spire of the south facade decayed, and in 1774 it was necessary to take them down. In 1828 architect William Strickland designed the extant tower, and this attractive belfry was often copied in public buildings and apartment houses.

Independence Hall is today a national shrine because it was here that the Declaration of Independence, the Articles of Confederation, and the Constitution were drafted and endorsed. These ground-breaking documents form the basis of our present legal and governmental systems.

Surrounded by skyscrapers, Independence Hall does not appear to be the momentous historical site that it is. But upon entering it, the visitor is quickly reminded of its importance. For before him stands the famous Liberty Bell which tolled the Declaration of Independence, and around him are the portraits of all those patriots who, in this place, carried out the letter of its inscribed message, "Proclaim Liberty throughout all the land unto the inhabitants thereof."

Diagram page 96

THE U.S. CAPITOL :: *"Here, the People Govern"*

Unquestionably one of the most elegant, modern, and serviceable houses of government, the United States Capitol building is also a highly recognizable symbol of power. Frequently heard and instantly understood are the implications of the phrase, "Today, at Capitol Hill...."

The cornerstone of the Capitol was laid in October 1793 by America's first chief-of-state, George Washington. Though the building itself was designed by an amateur architect, Dr. William Thornton (who won five hundred dollars and a city lot for his winning entry), presidents Washington, Jefferson, Adams, Lincoln, and statesmen Clay and Calhoun, and a host of other notable men over the years, all pitched in and "added a little something." It can honestly be said that all three branches of our Federal Government have had a hand in the Capitol's history. On the steps of the Capitol American presidents since Jackson have been inaugurated, and for 134 years the Capitol housed the Supreme Court as well as Congress.

Though the Capitol has been steadily enlarged and made more magnificent over the years, the oldest section is the rectangular North Wing, which presently connects the central Rotunda and the large Senate extension. Congress moved from the temporary capital of Philadelphia to hold its first Joint Session in the Capitol in late 1800. In the early 1800's the Capitol consisted of two basic structures connected by a primitive wooden walkway. Though the British burned the Capitol during the War of 1812 it was restored and a copper-coated wooden dome (today's is iron) set into place. During the Civil War, the enlarged Capitol served as a barracks, military hospital, and bakery. The physical plant of the Capitol, still "incomplete," occupies 131 acres, of which the building alone covers $3^1/2$. There are $16^1/2$ acres of floor space, over 540 rooms, 675 windows, a huge dome requiring over 1000 gallons of paint per year, miles of corridors, restaurants, stores, shops, offices, banking and medical facilities, press rooms, art galleries, Congressional meeting halls, and hundreds of smaller rooms including reception rooms, and dining areas. Columns of colorful marbles, jasper, and other handsome materials grace the arched hallways; ornately tiled floors are common, as are frescoes, murals, carvings, portraits, wood panels, and crystal chandeliers.

The decor of Congress is one of separation: the Senate chamber is traditionally red and gold, the House, blue. Some members occupy seats and tables of past heroes and orators whose names are carved in the wood. A lit red light above the main entrance is the signal that the House is in session, just as a lit white light indicates the Senate Executive Session, closed to the public.

Statuary Hall, one of the Capitol's showplaces, contains statues and busts of individual states' "favorite sons" and daughters. It is in this hall that visitors witness the Capitol's marvelous acoustical quality, as a guide's whispered message is heard across the hall with amazing clarity. Another favorite of visitors is the huge Rotunda with its dome, where great American statesmen and "soldiers of freedom" have lain in state on the traditional catafalque. The Capitol is one of America's proudest landmark possessions: "No Capitol in the world has done more to safeguard free democratic debate, the privileges of minorities, the fundamental civil liberties of man."

Diagram page 97

THE GOVERNOR'S PALACE ⁞⁞ *Colonial Willamsburg, Virginia*

From the cool stone figures of an English lion and a Scottish unicorn that guard the wrought-iron entrance gate, to the glittering ballroom, vast wine cellars and lush gardens, the Governor's Palace is Colonial Williamsburg's most elegant and imposing building. Reconstructed on its original foundations, the Palace was built to serve as a lasting symbol of the power and prestige of the British Crown in Colonial Virginia. But during its 74-year lifespan, the Palace also acted as a hospital for patriots in the American Revolution, and a fitting executive mansion for the first two governors of a free Virginia.

This impressive structure took quite a while to be built. For almost two decades before the capital of the colony moved from Jamestown to Williamsburg in 1699, each incoming royal governor had instructions from the Crown that directed the building of a governor's house. Work began in 1706. By 1718 so much money had been spent that the colonists began to refer to it derisively as "the Palace."

The Palace served as the official residence of seven royal governors. Since the governor's authority at that time stretched out to the Mississippi and up to the Great Lakes, social recognition at the Palace was the New World equivalent of acceptance at the Court of England. But the atmosphere changed drastically as the seeds of the Revolution germinated. Social gaiety in an attempt to humor the colonists turned to "haughty" and "supercilious" behavior on the part of a fearful governor, until the Earl of Dunmore fled the Palace before dawn one June morning in 1775.

After Dunmore's evacuation the new Commonwealth came into being, and the Palace served for five years as the executive mansion for governors Patrick Henry and Thomas Jefferson. In 1780 the capital moved to Richmond, and the governor's residence in Williamsburg served first as a military headquarters and then, during the Yorktown campaign, as a hospital. Unfortunately, the Palace did not survive the war. Three days before Christmas, the main residence burned to the ground.

Diligent research, however, has returned the Palace, its supporting buildings, and extensive gardens to their eighteenth-century appearance. Years of painstaking investigation by archaeologists, architects, curators, historians, and landscape architects culminated in 1934 with the recreation of the magnificence that characterized the Palace complex of two centuries ago. With the help of complete inventories taken after the deaths of two royal governors, a detailed sketch made by Thomas Jefferson, and the discovery of a remarkable etching called the "Bodlian Plate," it has been possible to recreate very closely how the Palace must have looked, inside and out. The eighteenth century lives again in all of Colonial Williamsburg. Two hundred years melt away as visitors walk through the Governor's Palace, the Capitol, Wetherburn's Tavern, the Courthouse and other historic sites. Nearly a mile in length, the Colonial area includes 88 original buildings, shops and homes which have been preserved and restored, and forty-eight other important structures which have been rebuilt on their original foundations. In this unique setting, Williamsburg's costumed hosts, hostesses, and craftsmen recall for thousands of visitors each year the importance of this colony, and how its inhabitants lived and worked.

Diagram page 98

D'EVEREUX ⠿ *Perfect Mirror to the Past*

D'Evereux, a fine example of Greek Revival and one of the most picturesque of Southern antebellum mansions, is nestled in the bluffs of Natchez, Mississippi, which overlooks the mighty Mississippi River. Founded by the French in 1716 and passing subsequently under English and Spanish rule, Natchez flourished with a society of graceful culture based on an enormous prosperity founded on cheap land, cotton, and labor. It became a sophisticated, pleasure-loving community where manners were as important as wealth, and both were present in abundance. In many ways this society was unique in America and it produced something quite distinctive in its architecture. Today the city of Natchez is a mecca for those wishing to travel back to the days of the Old South. Once a year, during the month of March, the Natchez Pilgrimage takes place, offering lovers of history and romantic tradition the opportunity to explore the lovely homes of Natchez, including D'Evereux.

From U.S. Highway 61 D'Evereux mansion's classic splendor stops the passerby of today much as it must have stopped the traveller of yesterday along the Natchez Trace. Chaste and spacious, this particular home's beauty lies in its six stately Doric columns, its delicate grilled balcony, its massive grandeur against rich and colorful gardens. Once inside, one quickly recognizes the characteristics of a typical Southern mansion. A capacious center hall spans the length of the house with rooms off to either side. The double parlors to the right are joined by large folding doors and have jib windows opening onto the front and rear galleries. Behind the dining room on the left of the hallway is a Jeffersonian stairwell opening off the hall, with a swing staircase bordered by a slender mahogany stair rail. This staircase connects the first and second floors with the attic and is paralleled by a service hallway and a large butler's pantry. On the second floor, four bedrooms open off a hallway which duplicates that on the first floor. Several original outbuildings are still standing, including the kitchen, the "young men's house," and the "necessary house."

Built for William St. John Elliot and his wife Anna Frances Conner the house was given Mr. Elliot's mother's family name. D'Evereux Hall, as it was originally called, was completed in 1840. Mr. and Mrs. Elliot enjoyed their magnificent home, entertaining a constant stream of guests, many of whom were national celebrities. While seeking the office of President of the United States, Henry Clay attended an affair there in his honor that has been called the grandest ball ever given in the state of Mississipi.

When Mr. Elliot died in 1855, he willed the house to the Catholic Church for an orphanage. Mrs. Elliot bought it back and lived there until 1876. She in turn willed D'Evereux to her 16-year-old great-niece, Margaret Martin (later Mrs. Bayard Shields). In 1925 Mrs. Shields sold the house to Virginia Smith, a schoolteacher from Chicago. Mrs. Smith began restoration of the house that year and in 1941, retired and came to take up residence. Upon Mrs. Smith's death, the house was willed to the University of Chicago, her alma mater, so it could be sold and the money used for scholarships. In June 1962 the T.B. Buckles family purchased D'Evereux and began a more extensive restoration. Today, D'Evereux's tall, graceful columns, broad galleries, spacious entranceways, and magnificent gardens offer a perfect mirror to the past.

Diagram page 99

THE FRENCH QUARTER ⠶ *New Orleans*

In the heart of New Orleans lies the quaint, historically rich French Quarter—the original Nouvelle Orleans. But this "Paris of the South," with its charming architecture, authentic French restaurants, and havens for Dixieland jazz, was once nothing more than a muggy, dismal cypress swamp. By 1717 the large French Province of Louisiana had been partially surveyed by the Canadian explorers Pierre and Jean Baptiste LeMoyne (Sieur de Bienville). The territory had been granted to successive parties who had hopes of reaping wealth from pearl fisheries and gold and silver mines. But Bienville found none of these treasures, and urged instead the development of agriculture in the rich lands of the Mississippi Valley and the establishment of a town along the River to handle the great volume of trade he foresaw for the future.

Bienville's ideas were not heeded by the enterprising companies attempting to exploit the territory, but in 1718, when he became governor of the Province, Bienville began to establish his proposed river town on a swampy crescent bend of the Lower Mississippi. With the assistance of the French engineer Adrien de Pauger, Bienville surveyed the site and laid out a parallelelogram measuring 4000 feet by 1800 feet—the area that today comprises the French Quarter (also known as *Vieux Carré*, the Old Square). The site was divided into 66 squares and each square was further divided into lots. Two large squares were reserved in the center: the Place d'Armes (now Jackson Square) for a parade ground, and an adjacent square for governmental and ecclesiastical buildings.

In 1722 New Orleans became the Provincial Capital and by 1727 the population doubled; the site was cleared of swamp, snakes, and alligators; and substantial shingled and whitewashed buildings appeared. In 1762 Louisiana Province came under Spanish rule and the city added another dimension to its developing character. Old World rule of New Orleans ended in 1803 when the United States purchased Louisiana Territory from France (which had reacquired it from Spain that same year). American settlers of the early 1800's established a community of their own opposite Canal Street, thus creating a distinct dividing line between old and new New Orleans.

Today the French Quarter is surrounded on one side by the skyscrapers of modern industry and on the other side by the Garden District (elaborate gardens and mansions dating from the great "cotton prosperity" of the South). The Colonial buildings that survive in the Quarter date from the Spanish period, for in 1794 great fires destroyed most of the original buildings. Very Old World in appearance, the buildings that remain are a strange mixture of French and Spanish design adapted to New Orleans' climate and topography. Most are built of brick covered with stucco to preserve the mortar from dampness. Their typically plain, pastel front walls are flush with the sidewalk and the back walls open out onto shrub and flower-laden patios and courtyards. Ornate iron-lace balconies and wrought-iron gates abound. The streets, lined with old lanterns, are narrow, their French/Spanish names paved into them in colorful tiles. In the Quarter, zoning laws (for historic preservation) are strictly enforced, but the quaint old buildings are still filled with life, for many have become nightclubs, bars, hotels, superb French restaurants (such as Antoine's, established in 1840), apartments, antique shops, and art galleries.

Diagram page 100

THE FARM IN THE HILL COUNTRY

By nature of its poverty in tillable land and its richness in pasture, the hill country has emerged as America's dairy land. Throughout New England and eastern New York State, spreading southward through Pennsylvania, Maryland, and Virginia, westward through parts of Ohio, Michigan, Indiana, and Illinois, to Wisconsin and Minnesota, and prominent in any other green and hilly section of the nation, the silos push upward among the rolling hills, poetic symbols of an industry whose keynote is discipline.

With few exceptions dairy farms are family enterprises, the women and children working as diligently as the men. The consumers of the nation could well hope the inhabitants of this farmstead in Pennsylvania never recognize how hard they labor for their daily bread. They are up at 5:00 for morning milking and sit down to supper at 7:30 or 8:00 when the milker is washed and the bulk tank is cooling the day's yield. Somewhere in between they fit the routine that belongs to their feed production and their cash-crop farming—tilling, planting, mowing, combining, silo filling.

The neat cluster of house, barns, and silos, the multicolored fields with their neat furrows, bespeak more than an occupation on the land. They represent a system of values, a proud heritage, a way of life. The family who farm this place have roots as deep as the alfalfa that grows in the pastures. Stop in for "dinner" at noon and they will show you the musket an ancestor carried in the Revolution, the Indian artifacts a succession of grandfathers gleaned from the land, and the bewhiskered portrait of the great-great-grandfather who fought at Gettysburg. You will discover too that for all its seeming isolation, there is a complexity to an American farm today that no picture can portray. At the end of the lane is a mailbox; up and down the valley are strung the farms of the neighbors; over the hill rises a church steeple, a village school, a state university; beyond all stretch the highways. All of these profoundly influence life on this farm in the hill country.

It would seem that these influences produce desirable results; yet each year hundreds of hill farmers sell their herds and fields and "throw in the towel" in the losing battle between rising costs and prices. The hill country farm is one of the more romantic elements of the American dream, but the dream is an elusive one. It is a somewhat sad and ironic fact that one of the finest products the American farm sends to the city year after year is its youth. "Golly, Dad," said the farmer's son climbing up and taking his first look from the top of the silo, "from up here you can see clear to Harrisburg!" And when he grew up, he migrated to Harrisburg. One can't help wondering if the view back to the farm was ever quite as clear.

There is a "farm mystique" engendered by deep roots and strong human ties; there is a hunger never filled, a longing never quieted that has its source in the farm in the hills.

Diagram page 101

"AMERICAN PATCHWORK" :: *Contoured Rhythm and Beauty*

Impressive vistas of America are the exclusive possession of the airborne—it isn't fair, but that's the way it is. Even the northeastern Iowa farmer who holds title to this broad acreage of the Mississippi watershed northwest of Dubuque can't appreciate its unique beauty as easily as the computer salesman flying from Milwaukee to Des Moines.

Anyone who flies over the prairies of the Midwest must acknowledge that the American heart beats to the rhythm of the square mile. (How will the square kilometer ever vanquish the square mile?) Here and there, however, the prairie is punctuated with rolling hills where farmers have risen to the challenge of producing crops and preserving their topsoil with the practice of contour farming. And in the patterns they form they defy the square mile. Fitting and planting a field crossways to a slope is an ancient phenomenon. An Aztec standing at the foot of the Andes in the wake of a gullywasher probably scratched his head and said, "Hey, man—our dirt is flowing down-hill!" and contouring began. But American farmers, spurred by the crisis of the Dustbowl era, advanced it to an artform. There is a precise formula for the width of these contour strips which relates to the steepness of the slope—thus the visual effect is one of geometric rhythm and beauty.

Strip cropping (as in our needlework) is a practice that is combined with contouring for minimum erosion. Strips of open-soil crops like corn or sorghum are alternated with strips of forage or hay crops that have extensive root systems to catch and hold the water. In long steep situations, a system of terracing is practiced with permanent grass waterways easing the water down and across hills to lower terraces.

The airplane and aerial photography are indispensable tools of the Agriculture Department's Soil Conservation Service, which has been extremely helpful to farmers in diagnosing and dealing with erosion and other problems. Drainage patterns, field sizes, crops, plant diseases, and plant nutrition can all be determined from the air. But these are agricultural facts best appreciated by the Iowa farmer. The patterns belong to the computer salesman, the Coast-bound executive, the fancy-free vacationer taking in the scene—who will, hopefully, appreciate the genius and skill of the men who bring this patchwork into being.

God hath wrought wonders, indeed. But looking down on the contour-tilled panoramas of southeastern Ohio, Kentucky, Tennessee, northern Alabama, southwestern Wisconsin or any of many others in the United States, one must be awed by what man has added.

HIGH LAKE NEAR TELLURIDE

The magnificent Colorado Rockies abound with delightful natural surprises. This view of lofty snow-capped peaks from High Lake, near the historic mining town of Telluride, typifies the scenic wonders of the region. The traveler heading west from the town of Gunnison, for example, will have little idea of the variety of sights which will greet him on the road to Telluride.

First comes a stretch of relatively flat, slightly rolling country with sparse vegetation and an occasional ranch house and cattle pen complex along the highway. It is hard to believe one is already well over a mile above sea level! Now the road takes on a slight grade as it winds into the low hills around the huge Blue Mesa Reservoir, a popular recreation area as well as a vital source of water. Even the raw, man-made look the reservoir still retains cannot spoil the growing beauty of the surrounding country. Then onward through the small town of Cimarron, towards the local agricultural center, Montrose. Perhaps we will take a side trip here to tour the Black Canyon of the Gunnison National Monument, where the Gunnison River has cut a channel so steep, so deep, and so narrow that the sun cannot reach the bottom. At Montrose, we turn south. Again we are riding through a broad valley, this one more cultivated. And again the land inches upward as we aim towards Ouray, another famous mining camp, now a thriving tourist center in the midst of Uncompahgre National Forest.

The road takes on a steeper grade, winding up the sides of the peaks—now we are in the mountains for certain. In the valley far below is a river. On both sides of the road, pine trees and aspen crowd the view. The air is cool, dry, and sweet. Its thinness (and the way we gasp for breath when we walk) hints at high altitude. The sun is warm, but stepping into the shade for even a few minutes can bring a chill. Little breezes spring up, gust quickly in all directions, and disappear. The trees hiss and roar in their wake. The breezes bring the smell of pine and earth.

The climb to Telluride continues, weaving ever upward. Taking the turnoff to High Lake, we travel through pine forest, but as we continue our journey, the trees become fewer and farther between. We are approaching timberline, above which only tough grasses and surprisingly delicate wildflowers can grow. We make the final turn, and before us lies the lake, picture-postcard pretty...a deep blue, slightly rippled by the wind. There are no beaches on these mountain lakes; the grass grows down to the water, which will be ice-cold, fed by snowbanks. It will never warm up much, because the summers here are short and cool. Behind the lake lies the natural wonder that dominates this part of the world. Arching thousands of feet above us are the mountains, breathtaking in their beauty. This lake, already two miles above sea level...how is it possible for these peaks to scale still more craggy altitude?

It is the same feeling later, when we go to Telluride itself. A neat, rain-washed village—a thriving ski resort in winter— the old mining camp never looked better, with remodeled gingerbread houses painted bright colors. But even the jaunty community is no match for the mountains that tower above it. This is the true grandeur of the Rockies. While the lake is beautiful and the town is pleasant, either could be almost anywhere. It is the aching massiveness of the mountains crowding close that gives High Lake and Telluride their special character.

Diagram page 103

THE ST. GEORGE TEMPLE ∷ *Gem of Utah's "Dixie"*

Located in Utah's St. George Valley, the St. George Temple occupies a commanding position on a six-acre plot in the southeastern section of the city. The first Mormon temple to be erected in the western United States, it stands today as a monument to the robust faith of the stouthearted pioneers who settled the region. Mormons first came to the St. George area in 1857 to establish a "cotton mission" in Washington County to supply the territory with cotton. Many of these families were Southern converts to the Church, a fact which contributed greatly to the nickname of "Dixie" later given to the area.

Brigham Young proposed construction of a temple in St. George in 1871, and the Mormons of Utah's "Dixie," eager to have a permanent house of worship, voted to undertake the task. Building a temple on the wilderness plains of southern Utah, far from other settlements, was not easy. Workmen ran into difficulty from the beginning. Water seeped into the foundation excavations and threatened to halt work. The hardy Mormons drained the water from the site and devised a crude "pile driver" from an old Mexican war cannon filled with lead to pound thousands of tons of black volcanic rock into the earth as a firm base for the foundation. The work was slow, sometimes just a few feet a day, but as the site was made secure from further seepage, the masons laid the foundation of great slabs of malipi blocks. Hidden drains were engineered to direct some water inside the temple for lavatories and for the baptismal font, and to direct unneeded and refuse water away from the temple area. This ingenious drainage system still functions perfectly today.

Workmen laid up the outside walls of red sandstone from local quarries and plastered them with sparkling white stucco. Teamsters hauled lumber eighty miles by oxcart from Mt. Trumbill's steam sawmill and other pineries. Carpenters fastened heavy hand-hewn timbers with wooden pegs for roof beams, and skilled craftsmen fashioned spiral staircases and carved delicate interior woodwork. The remarkable baptismal font of the temple weighs 18,000 pounds and rests on the backs of 12 cast-iron oxen symbolic of the 12 tribes of Israel from which Mormons believe they are descended. It was designed and manufactured in Salt Lake City by English iron molders who had been converted to the Church. The pieces of the font were hauled 318 miles from Salt Lake City to St. George by three ox teams and welded together at the temple site. From his winter home in St. George, Brigham Young was periodically able to oversee the building operation. Under his direction, and after nearly six years of struggle, and nearly one million dollars in donations of labor, materials, foodstuffs, clothes, and money, the edifice was dedicated on April 6, 1877—less than five months before the death of Brigham Young.

The building measures 114 feet by 93 feet, with outside walls rising 84 feet from foundation to castellated parapets, 175 feet to the topmost vane. Major renovations and the addition of annex buildings in 1937—38 and 1974—75 introduced modern furnishings and facilities. The temple's exterior lines, however, still reflect the Gothic Revival design elements apparent in other nineteenth-century temples in Salt Lake City, Manti, and Logan, Utah.

Diagram page 104

THE MISSION AT CARMEL

An important and colorful part of the development of what is now California, the Spanish mission system flourished in New Spain (Baja and Upper California) between 1770 and 1820. Although permanent Spanish settlement had been established in lower California in the early 1600's, colonization of Upper California was not a serious concern until the 1760's, when the Russians and British became a threat to Spanish mining towns in the north. Thus in 1769 four expeditions left Baja California by land and sea, for the port of Monterey. The Franciscan Junipero Serra (the Grey Ox) was part of a land expedition which established the mission San Carlos de Borromeo de Monterey on June 3, 1770. This mission, five miles from Monterey at Carmel, became the northernmost terminal of the road from lower California, and the headquarters for Father Serra and the California missions.

The Spanish method of colonization was to establish threepart units along the frontier, each unit consisting of a mission; a pueblo, or planned civilian village; and a presidio, or military fortress. Twenty-one such missions and their associated institutions were to be set up from Monterey to San Diego. Franciscan friars, wearing robes of grey sackcloth and broad, wide-brimmed hats, set out to establish the missions "a day's walking journey apart" along a coastal path that would become known as *El Camino Real*—"The King's Highway." The Franciscans were among the best educated men of their day—trained not only to teach religion, but carpentry, masonry, smithing, and the many tasks of farming. With great zeal, the friars lured the Indians to the missions. Many Indians "cooperated" in return for food, the promise of salvation, and protection from the Spanish military.

The missions grew from small, mud-smeared log structures into sprawling plantations. Built in a quadrangle around a patio, they included long, low buildings for the friary, a dormitory for Indians, soldiers, and servants; a kitchen, workshops, storage bins and granaries. Each mission developed a strong individuality and was known for its friars, its wealth, its size, or its beauty. But together the missions became the economic lifeblood of the province.

Thus the missions prospered for nearly fifty years. But when Mexico won its independence from Spain in 1821 and California pledged its allegiance to the new Republic, secularization of the missions became a burning issue. In August 1833 the Mexican Government passed a Secularization Act under which half the holdings of each mission would be turned over to the State and the other half divided among the Indians capable of living on their own. The administrators who assumed control in California ignored the intentions of the Mexican Congress, however, and divided the fertile mission lands and herds among their own favorites. By 1840 all the missions had been secularized and plundered. Many of the Franciscans left California, the 30,000 mission Indians were set adrift, and the buildings of the mission chain abandoned. The mission at Carmel lay in ruin until the 1880's, when extensive restoration was begun on the complex. Today the mission stands as a beautiful, functioning Minor Basilica, nestled among the cypress trees. A red-tiled roof covers the buildings; the tower is of Moorish design; the lime-washed sandstone walls of the church—five feet thick—curve in a parabolic arch to the ceiling. Many original paintings and statues grace the interiors.

Diagram page 105

SANTA BARBARA'S SPANISH CASTLE ⠆⠆ *The County Courthouse*

A visiting Prince of Bourbon once described Santa Barbara as "the most Spanish city outside of Spain," and its county courthouse an equal to any castle in Seville. This distinction is rooted in over four centuries of tradition.

The first white men to lay eyes on the site of the future city of Santa Barbara arrived in 1542, just fifty years to the month after Columbus' discovery of the New World. These Spanish *conquistadores* were struck by the resemblance of the area to the Riviera: both have coastlines that run east and west. Mapmakers were later to learn that on the entire west coast of the New World, from the Aleutians to Panama and on to Cape Horn, the only east-west traverse of coastline was the fifty-mile stretch along the Santa Barbara Channel east of Point Conception. It was because of this unique geographical feature that the Spaniards found the largest concentration of prehistoric Indians in California in the Santa Barbara area, so it was far from coincidental that King Carlos III elected to build the last military outpost in New Spain here in 1782. Four years later, Santa Barbara's far-famed "Queen of the Missions" was established, now visited by thousands of tourists annually.

Yankee seafaring men began trading at Santa Barbara around 1800, swapping merchandise for cowhides and tallow which they took around the Horn to the boot factories and candlemakers of Boston. When the Americans seized California from Mexico in 1847, Lt. John Charles Fremont ran up the Stars and Stripes at the Royal Presidio of Santa Barbara. The Gold Rush erupted a year later, and in 1850 California became the 31st star in Old Glory. Slowly, Santa Barbara began its metamorphosis from a drowsy Mexican pueblo into a bustling American frontier town with saloons, gambling halls, and Wells-Fargo stagecoaches.

In 1874 a granite courthouse was erected near the site of the old presidio ruins, a typical midwestern building with massive Corinthian columns under a gilded Roman dome. This edifice collapsed in the earthquake of June 29, 1925, which destroyed most of Santa Barbara's ramshackle clapboard houses but spared ancient adobes. Out of the dust-smoking ruins was to rise a picturesque California garden-city with architecture patterned after its original Hispanic heritage. When the time came to build a new courthouse on the site of the old, the taxpayers received a providential windfall: a major oil field came into being a few miles west of the city in 1928. The taxes paid by the discovery well alone amounted to $1,500,000 that first year—and this money was invested in what is regarded by architects as perhaps the most beautiful public building in America.

Occupying a city block and enclosing three sides of a square, the Santa Barbara County Courthouse resembles a fairy-tale Spanish castle, replete with tiled towers, stained-glass windows, wrought iron work, hewn beams, and more than 100,000 imported Algerian tiles. The square clock tower is surmounted by an observation platform commanding grand vistas of the roundabout city, its mountain backdrop, the sea and islands on the far horizon. Santa Barbara's world-famous Sunken Garden, bracketed by the crenellated parapets of the courthouse, is the scene of fandangos every August during the week of the full moon when the city presents its Old Spanish Days Fiesta, making the visitor forget he is in California or the U.S.A....

Diagram page 106

CROOKED, LOVELY LOMBARD STREET ⠐ *San Francisco*

San Francisco embodies every city's romantic dream of itself—that of a cool, elegant, worldly seaport whose steep streets offer breathtaking views of a beautiful bay. One of the steepest—and crookedest—streets in the city is Lombard Street, which winds its serpentine way near Telegraph Hill. This brick-paved road corkscrews down the slope between Hyde Street and Leavenworth in a series of almost ninety-degree turns—you have to be a skilled driver or a good walker to negotiate it successfully. Steps instead of sidewalks line the S-curves of this unusual residential street, which the local inhabitants navigate with aplomb. Lombard Street is a colorful sight, zigging and zagging through the brilliant hydrangea bushes that Park Commissioner Peter Bercut inspired his neighbors to plant. It may be one of the crookedest streets in the world, but it is also one of the loveliest.

Thanks to the pioneer city planners' preference for a squared-off grid, most of San Francisco's downtown streets march intrepidly up steep hills, terrifying newly arrived drivers and making cable cars more than mere sentimental anachronisms. But this only adds to the city's charm, which turns nearly every tourist's visit into a lasting romance. Warmed by a congenial sun and washed in fresh Pacific breezes, this city of precipitous hills stretches seven miles across in each direction, rimmed on three sides by the sea. Its awe-inspiring bay, 450 square miles, is a natural gateway to the Orient that helped make San Francisco a melting pot of Occidental and Oriental. San Francisco's lusty history began when early Portuguese, English, and Spanish explorers penetrated the bay. In 1775 the Spanish ship *San Carlos* sailed through the Golden Gate to drop the first anchor off San Francisco.

On March 28, 1776, a mission site was selected and dedicated to St. Francis of Assisi. The little village of Yerba Buena developed near the mission, slumbering until 1836 when it grew into an important trading post.

In 1846, Captain John B. Montgomery and 70 men came ashore from the U.S.S. *Portsmouth* and hoisted the Stars and Stripes, marking the end of Mexican rule. The next year the village changed its name to San Francisco. A year later, gold was discovered in Sutter's millrace—an event that had tremendous impact on San Francisco. As the news spread around the world, a torrent of people and ships descended on the city, filling it with rough, tough transients and a good share of vice and violence. Hungry for gold, the East was also migrating to California. With the aid of imported Chinese labor, 2,000 miles of railroad tracks crossed the nation's two greatest mountain ranges to join east and west. Shipping to the Orient flourished and small industries prospered.

San Francisco spent the last half of the 19th century as part frontier town, part growing metropolis—struggling to reform its ills. Then on April 18, 1906, came the great earthquake and fire which wiped out the entire business area and burned out 497 blocks of buildings in the heart of the city. Losses amounted to 500 lives and $350 million. With the ashes still warm, the city gamely started a rebuilding which was largely completed by 1919.

San Francisco is now the third most important financial center in the U.S. and a hub of culture. In all tourist adventures, San Francisco is rivaled only by New York. A city whose many visitors verify what Gene Fowler once said, "Every man should be allowed to love two cities—his own and San Francisco."

Diagram page 107

THE NEW YORK WATERFRONT :: *Place of Beginnings*

When Verrazano and Hudson first sailed it, the New York waterfront of ocean and rivers and bays was in its primeval state. The land, inhabited by Algonquin subtribes—Wappingers and Delawares—was heavily forested, and the water abounded with fish. The harbor was a refuge from the severe North Atlantic storms, a haven which rarely froze over and was protected from the ocean's winter fog.

The New York waterfront was one of the first areas in the New World to be populated. Under the Dutch and the English, sailing ships brought in settlers and manufactured goods, and carried raw materials back to Europe. Many waterways and settlements in the New York area still bear their early Dutch names.

Later, at the time of the Boston Tea Party, New Yorkers, too, showed their sentiments and blocked the harbor so tea-laden British vessels could not dock. During the Revolutionary War the waterfront became an important strategic stronghold. New York divided the rest of the colonies geographically. If the British could hold it, the revolutionaries would be cut off from each other and their supplies, and British men-of-war from the harbor could effectively block north or south bound ships. If the British had prevailed, American history would be a different story.

In the new American nation, the waterfront grew as a center of mercantile activity. With more than 750 miles of navigable waterway available, business and industry progressed around the bustling port. Ships brought in goods from many parts the world, but the most precious cargo of all was people.

It was the people of many countries, those who dreamed and would work to fulfill their dreams, who built this land. Most of them began their new life in this country at the New York waterfront. As many as 30,000 people from all over the world arrived there in one day during the peak of immigration.

Once the most famous and grandiose ships on the New York waterfront were the great passenger liners. But in the age of air travel, the life of the docks are the cargo ships, two-thirds of which are arriving from or bound for foreign ports. Daily they bring in oil and gas, rubber, motor vehicles, lumber, textiles, hides, pharmaceuticals, footwear, flour, fruit, sugar, coffee, tea, liquors, lead, zinc, and copper ore, to name but a very few. Sixteen different rail lines and more than 10,000 trucks per day carry goods to and from the ships. It is no wonder that New York has become the financial capital of the world.

As the sightseer approaches New York by water, he may be momentarily distracted by the tugboats and barges that travel the waterways. He may be amazed at the vast oil tankers resting at anchor, or the beautiful bridges spanning the waterways. But the truly arresting sight is the waterfront itself, for virtually from the water's edge, the skyscrapers rise. Far higher than the treetops of Hudson's era, the buildings attest to the monumental work carried on by the people, and the greatness of the vast natural harbor.

The tourist in New York often visits the Statue of Liberty, a proud landmark on Liberty Island in the center of the harbor. From that vantage point he can see this view of Lower Manhattan—which includes "the financial district," and the lofty "twin towers" of the World Trade Center operated by the Port Authority of New Jersey and New York. This 107-story complex includes the highest restaurant and open-air observation deck in the world. In the right forefront can be seen Battery Park (a military installation in earlier days) and the slips of the famed Staten Island Ferry. At the extreme right can be seen a glimpse of Brooklyn.

The viewer is reminded that all of Manhattan is indeed an island surrounded by the Hudson, East, and Harlem Rivers—and that the famed "skyline" of New York is ever-changing, but always impressive.

LAS VEGAS ⠿ *Uninhibited Action Town*

Wildly flashing, glittering neon looms for miles along the otherwise desolate desert floor. Las Vegas is awesome, lively, exciting—a place where days blend unnoticed into nights and back into days—where a last nickel is as important as a last million—where nearly every nook and cranny boasts superstar entertainment around the clock. Las Vegas—the "uninhibited action town"—but it wasn't always so....

As late as 1776 the area that was to become Las Vegas lay undisturbed by man, except for the native Paiute Indians. In this sun-scorched wilderness of rock and sand, only occasional meadows and springs offered respite. Soon, however, expeditions advanced along the Old Spanish Trail toward the Las Vegas Valley in an attempt to establish a trade route between Santa Fe and the missions of California. By 1830 caravans were using the trail and by 1850 Las Vegas was an established camping ground enroute from Salt Lake City to California.

In 1855 a group of Mormons arrived with the dual purpose of building a fort to protect the immigrants and the U.S. mail and of teaching the Indians agriculture. These early pioneers cleared the land, built a stockade, hauled logs from the western mountains, erected cabins, a dam, and planted crops. Families followed the pioneers; schools and a post office were established. But the Paiutes were not amenable to the Mormons' missionary efforts and in 1857 the settlement was abandoned, except for occasional use by riders carrying the overland mail. Thereafter for a short time, the land was privately owned and operated as a ranch. Then, in 1903, the settlement was bought by representatives of the proposed San Pedro, Los Angeles, Salt Lake Railroad. Las Vegas, the town, was thus officially born in 1905 when the railroad company offered lots for sale, with promises of municipal improvements and employment opportunities. Within two days a "town" appeared—of tents and half-built structures. The company fulfilled its promises and for years the little railroad town existed unnotoriously in the middle of the desert.

Then, in the early 1930's (and eight miles from Las Vegas) the Federal Government began construction on Hoover Dam (and Boulder City, designed to house the workers for the Dam). A Federal town, Boulder City allowed no gambling or sale of liquor, and workers thus began to frequent the sleepy town of Las Vegas in search of night life and entertainment. Small gambling houses sprang up and Las Vegas began to take on a new look. Developers bought up huge chunks of the surrounding sand and sagebrush, and soon Las Vegas became a boom town.

In the mid-1940's, big time, free-spending, free-wheeling—and sometimes questionable—operators arrived. Huge, even grotesque casinos with lavish, attention-getting floor shows and flashing signs appeared, most famously along a $3^1/_2$ mile length of U.S. 91, better known as The Strip. Here and elsewhere in the city rose such monuments to the games of chance as The Sands, The Dunes, The Flamingo, Caesar's Palace, The Desert Inn, and The Sahara.

In the late 1960's and early 70's, new corporate giants settled into Las Vegas and bought large areas of land and controlling interests in many casinos. Attempts were made to change the image of Las Vegas from an "uninhibited action town" to a family resort. But the veritable home of the slot machine, roulette, and crap tables would not be changed. There's always a chance to make that one lucky throw of the dice, spin of the wheel, turn of a card....

Diagram page 110

THE SOUTHWEST DESERTS ⠇⠇ *Life and History Abound*

The deserts of the Southwest (there are four) spread their awesome landscapes from southwest Texas to southeastern California, down from Utah far into northern Mexico. A traveller passing through this vastness of burning noonday heat and chilling night might well think these deserts cruel and lifeless. But life and history abound. Flora and fauna in amazing variety are here and mankind through the centuries not only wandered their length and breadth, but made them his home.

A desert has been defined as a region of deficient and uncertain rainfall. Desert colors during dry periods are those of sandy wastes, red mesas, far purple mountains, and turquoise sky. With the coming of spring and summer rains, the earth is spread with an even more marvelous tapestry of color. Plant life abounds in a great diversity from flowering grasses to giant cacti. In southern and western Arizona are the spectacular stands of Saguaro cacti towering up to fifty feet in height. Here also is the unique Ocotillo (Flaming Sword), its long, unbranching stems tipped with fiery red bloom in late spring. Perhaps the best known of the cacti throughout the deserts are the many species of flat-jointed Prickly Pear, or Beaver Tail cactus. Their flowers, yellow or magenta, are large and spectacular and the juicy red fruits that follow are eaten by animals, birds, and people. The grey-green foliage of Brittlebush (Incensio) covers rocky slopes, brightening the early spring landscape with masses of yellow flowers. Of the multitude of small flowering plants one of the most pleasing is the Sand Verbena that spreads its purple-pink carpets across the deserts in spring and early summer.

As varied and fascinating as the plant life are the many animal, bird, and reptile inhabitants. From pocket mouse to desert bighorn, elf owl to turkey buzzard, horned toad to sidewinder, all have evolved physical characteristics and habits quite different from similar species living in less harsh habitats.

Man also found a home in the desert. The early hunters of twelve thousand years ago slowly progressed through prehistoric Basketmaker and pottery-making cultures into later agrarian groups to the present desert Pueblos and tribes. In the early 1500's the first Europeans appeared. Spanish explorers and friars began to trace trails through trackless wastes, northward and westward from bases in Mexico. For nearly two centuries before the Declaration of Independence, the Trail of the Padres brought those who established missions and settlements. In 1776 Padre Francisco Garcés and Franciscan friars Dominguez and Escalante traversed the desert to cross the gorge of the Grand Canyon.

After 1800 history begins to crowd the deserts with crossings. In 1846 the Army of the West marched from New Mexico to California, and the 1849 Gold Rush brought thousands to desert routes. Cattle trails, wagon roads, and later, rail lines, opened the desert further to the push of civilization. Mexican territory became American, settlements grew to cities, and the deserts were found to be a place for living and delight by new populations.

Diagram page 111

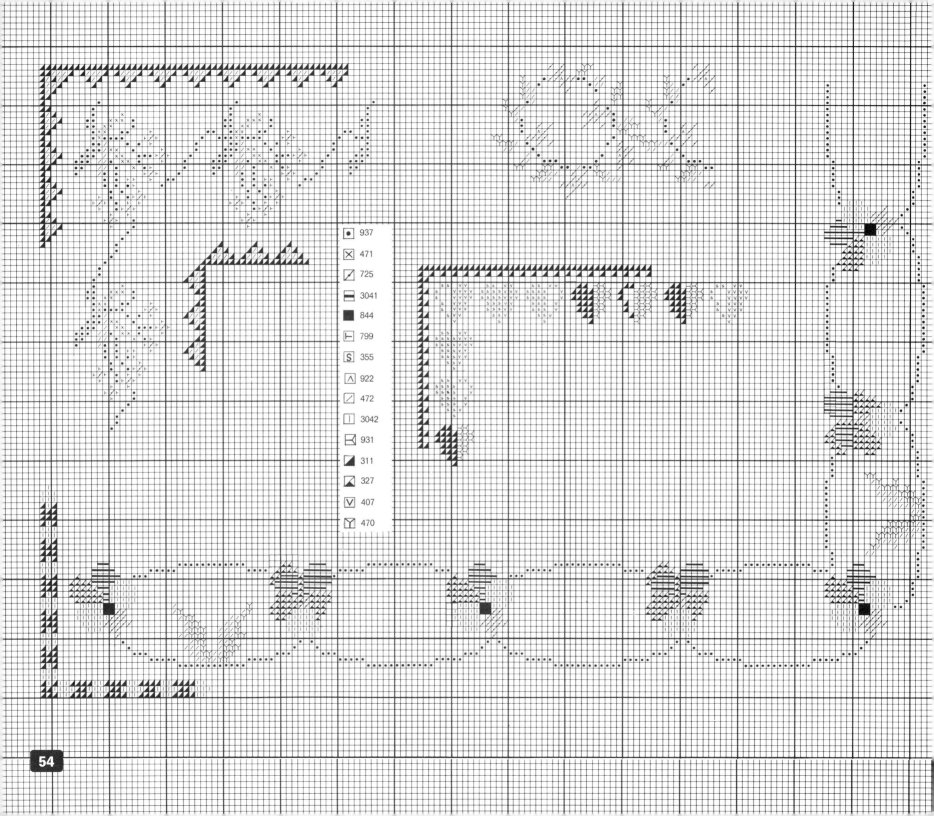

Symbol	Color
●	937
⊠	471
⁄	725
⊟	3041
■	844
⊢	799
S	355
∧	922
⁄	472
⫙	3042
⊟	931
◣	311
◤	327
V	407
Y	470

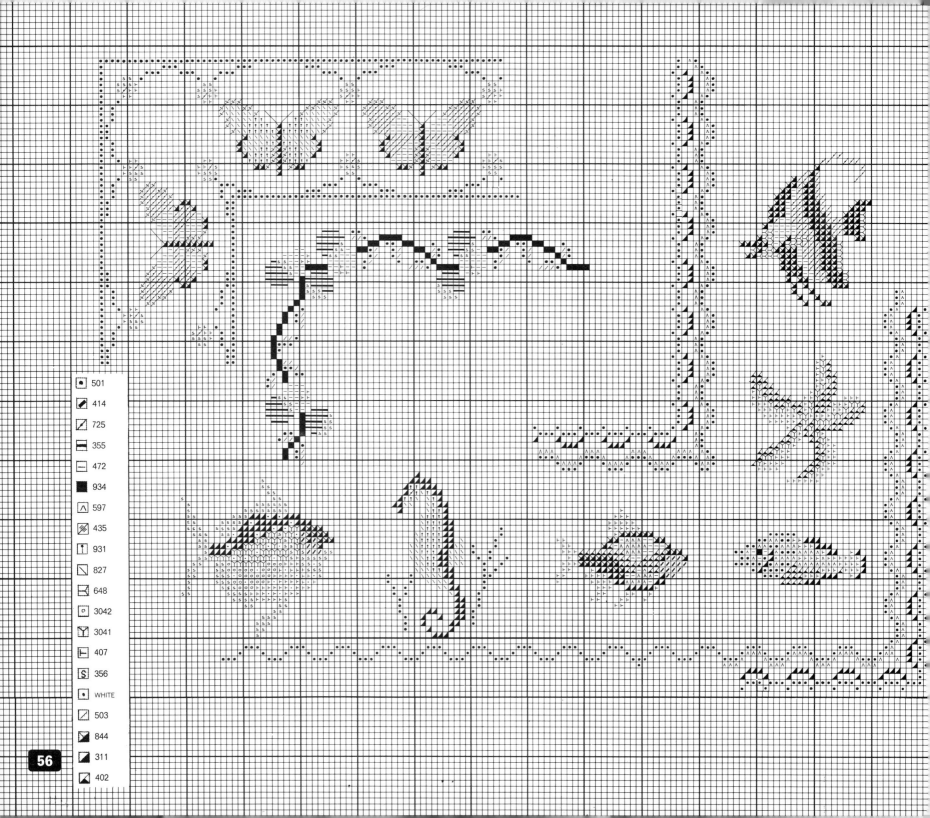

●	501
◪	414
◨	725
⊟	355
⊟	472
◼	934
△	597
▨	435
⊺	931
◻	827
◩	648
○	3042
⊻	3041
⊢	407
S	356
●	WHITE
◿	503
◪	844
◢	311
◺	402

56

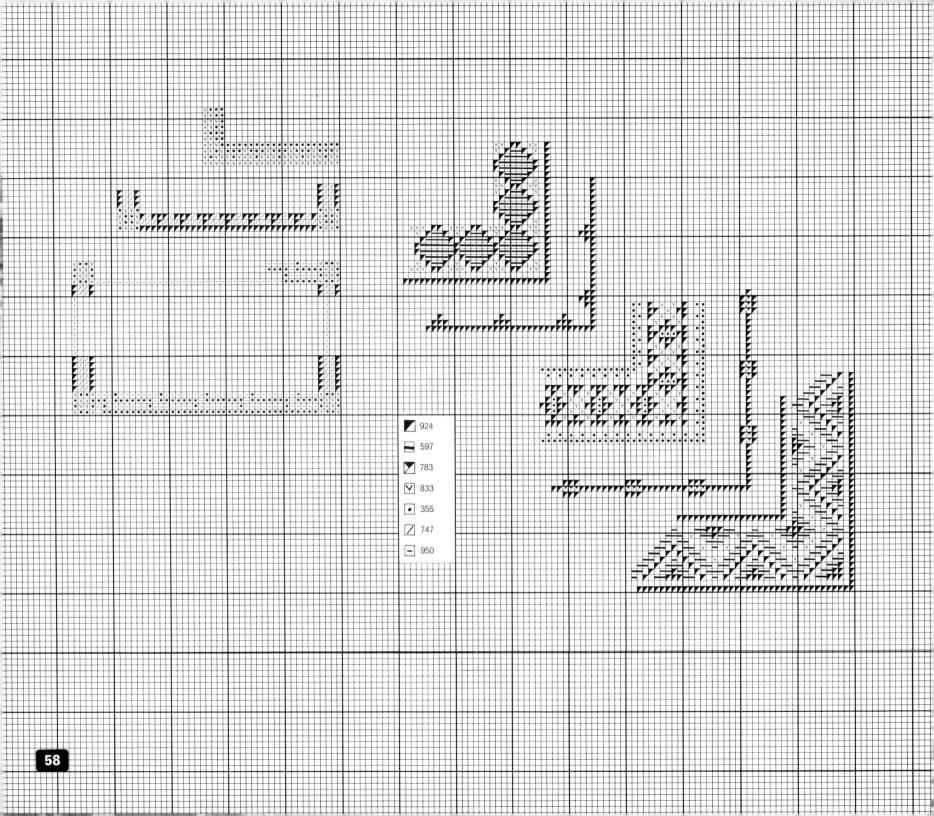

	924
	597
	783
	833
	355
	747
	950

58

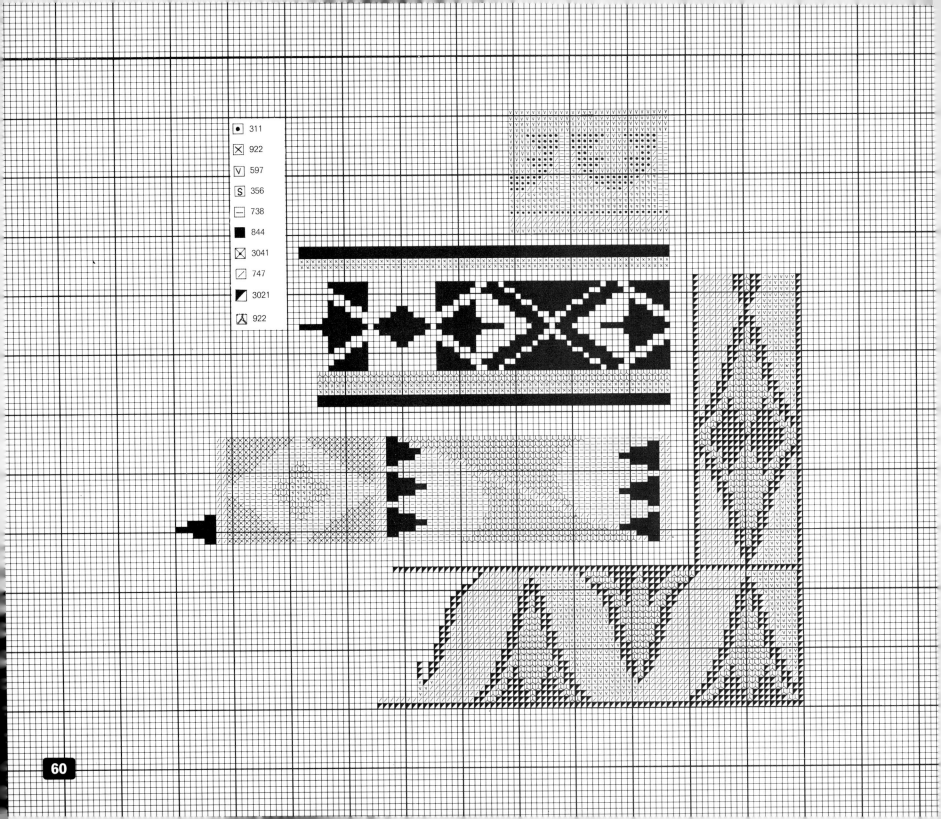

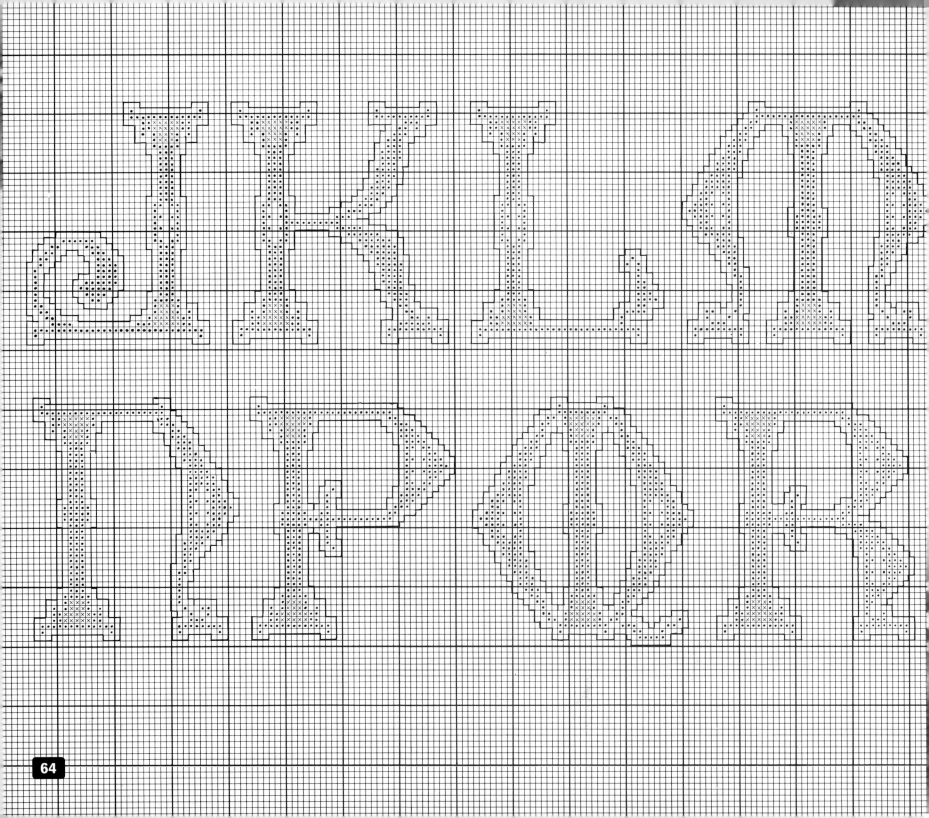

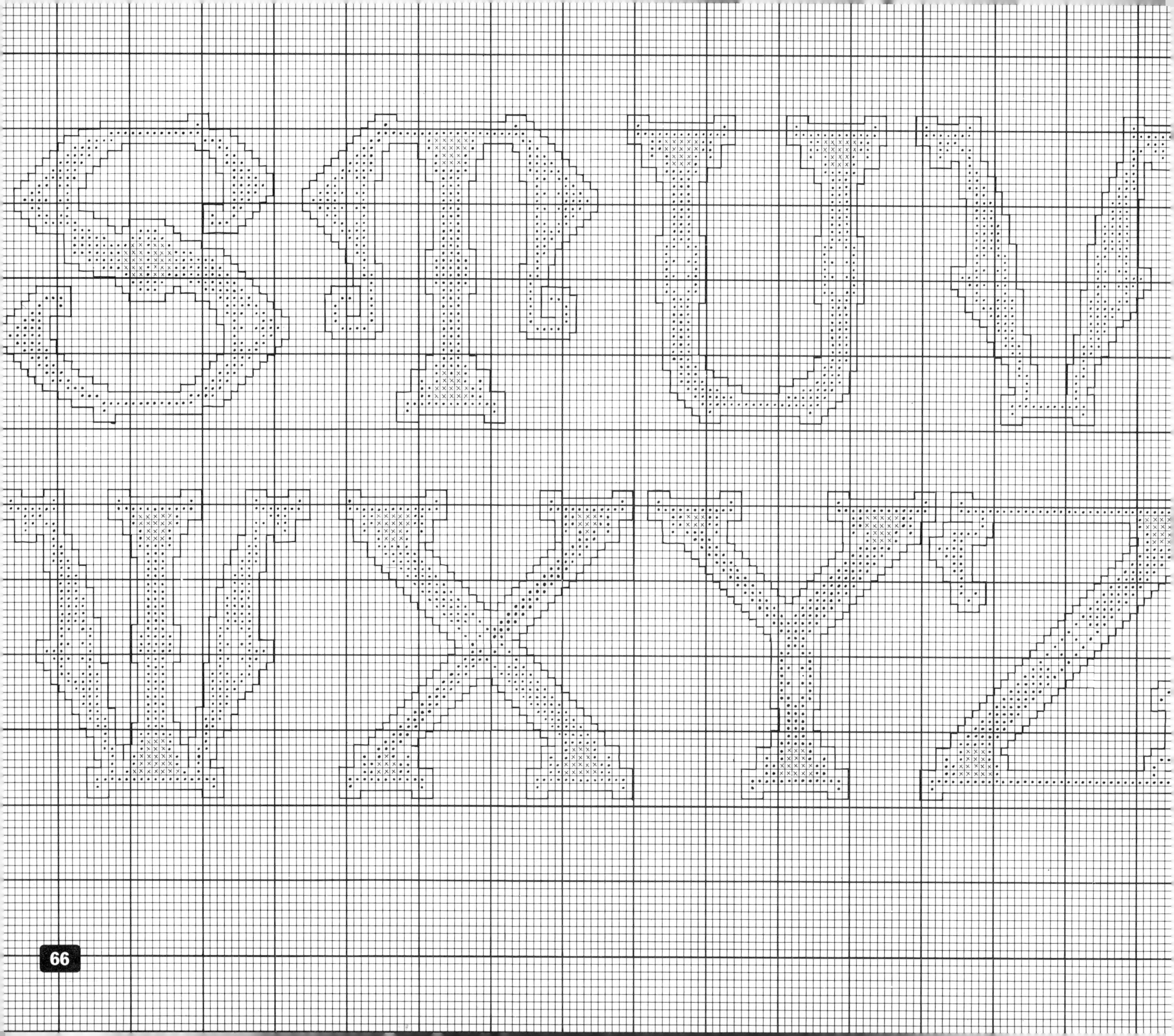

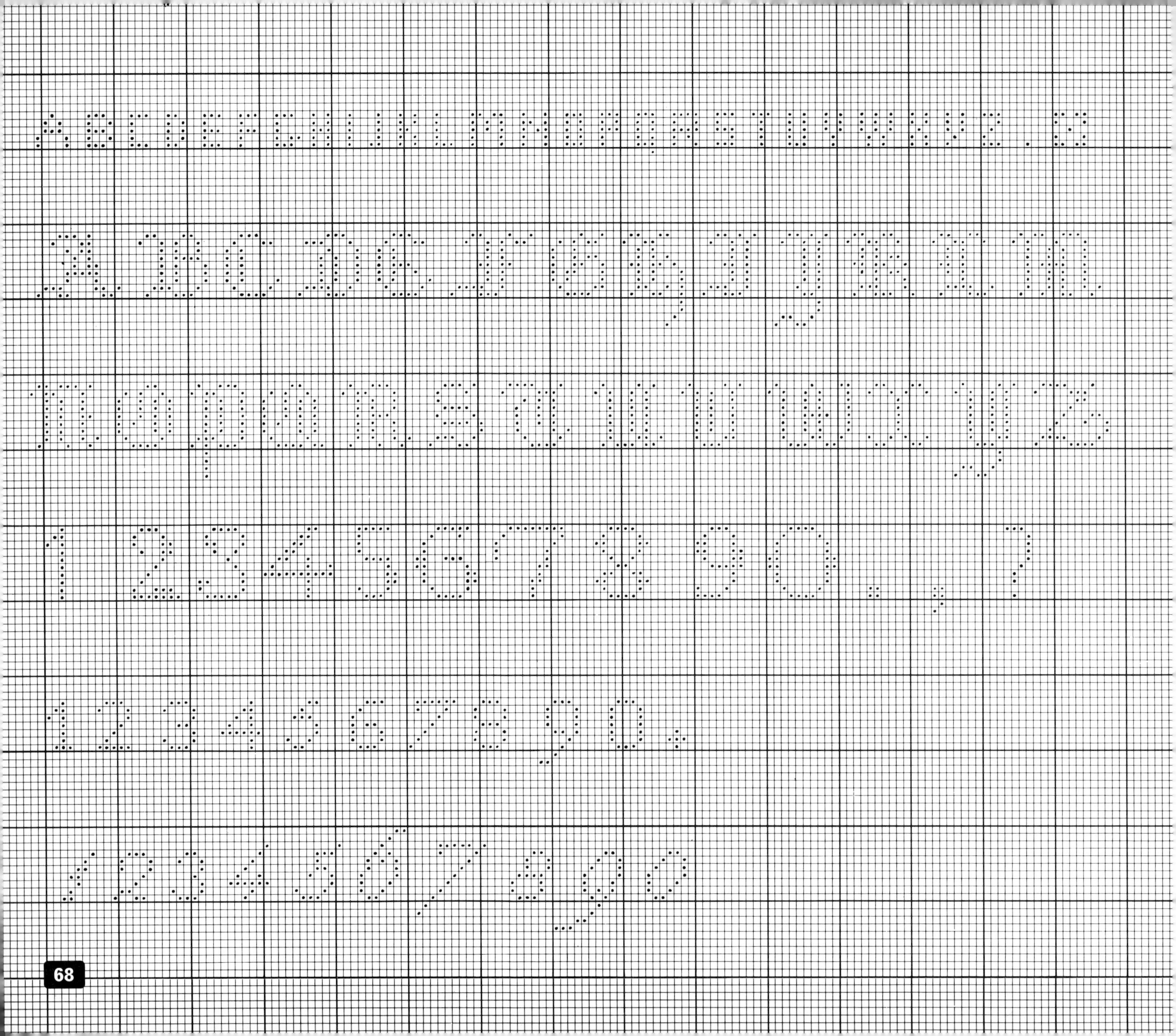

ABCDEFGHIJKLMNOPQRSTUVWXYZ.□

ABCDEFGHIJKLM
NOPQRSTUVWXYZ

1 2 3 4 5 6 7 8 9 0 . , ?

1234567890.1234567890

Notes and Instructions

On Symmetry

The world around us is filled with objects. Some of them are purely natural, others are man-made.

Looking at the living world, one thing is clear: there is no perfect symmetry in nature. No tree, plant, flower, or even single leaf can be cut in two identical halves. The same is true of animals and human beings. You need only compare your own two hands, or think of that pair of shoes, the right one fit so well but the left was a horror! Even the two parts of a seashell are not *precisely* alike in shape, size, and color. Although not scientifically proven, I daresay that perfect symmetry kills life, at least the "feeling" of life.

In olden days, before we had all our machinery, everything was made by hand. Although artisans strived for perfection, they never reached the same level of exactness and uniformity that modern machines do. This may very well be one of the reasons we love old and antique things. They give us a feeling of being alive, thus belonging to the living world. If we were faced with only mechanically-made things, if nature had nothing more in its pocket for us, we would have a terribly dead world!

But... there is always the light, shaping and reshaping all the objects we try to make so desperately alike. Light and shadow take away perfect symmetry, changing our artificial world into more liveable surroundings.

Thus stated, it is obvious that the use of light and shadow is necessary to all of the arts that attempt to reproduce "life."

The embroidery of Independence Hall can be used as an example. At first sight this building is of a perfect symmetry: the left and right sides have exactly the same windows, door, little windows, clock and tower are on the central line, and even the two arches are alike. In total darkness this would be true (although we would not be able to see it). As soon as the sun rises the shape comes out, we see the building. From now on the symmetry is broken. For as the day goes on the sun "moves," thus casting different shadows, according to the direction the sunlight is coming from. In this design the "light" comes from the right side, creating the shadows on the left side of outstanding parts. The same is true for the tower: the left side has to be darker than the right.

This principle can be found in all the other designs, most prominently when buildings constitute the main part of the design. Sometimes a simple dark line can make the difference between a dead and a living picture. The use of colors in this matter we will discuss in "On Color."

Another result of this "light game" is the fact that we "learn" whether something is round or square. On a round object the light goes fluently from one side to the other, while it "breaks off" on square objects. A round tower needs a different type of shading than a square one does.

If you should like to investigate this on your own, it may be helpful, especially when the light is very bright, to peep through your eyelashes. For me this game adds something essential to my perception of the world around me. I hope it will give you the same pleasure.

On Color

Color is probably the most important factor in the visual world. In fact, we cannot live without it. People who have to spend lengths of time in the Antarctic take along green plants to live with, to avoid a kind of blindness that comes from always seeing only white. Color is largely the means by which we recognize things, and distinguish their shapes. At dusk, when colors disappear, it becomes difficult to judge form and distance.

Anyhow, this book would be impossible without the use of colors! In the first place color tells us something about the object we are dealing with. Grass is green (or yellow, and by then we know something about the weather), a brick house is reddish, and the sky blue, grey, rose, or white (and thus we learn something about the weather and the time of day). The knowledge of whether a far-off mountain is covered with snow, trees, or grass depends upon the colors we see. In a way we react instinctively to colors. Who has not been a bit excited to think they are finding a precious stone or wildflower, only to find out when closer it was nothing more than a thrown-away piece of plastic!

Making the designs for this book, I tried to choose the colors as close as possible to reality. Although white and black may not officially be called colors (black is the lack of color while white is the total sum of all colors), for our purposes we shall add them to the list.

Starting with the colors of the rainbow: red, orange, yellow, green, blue, indigo, and violet, all kinds of mixtures can be made. Natural colors most of the time are such mixtures;

moreover, one tree or flower may contain so many shades of just green or blue, that it is impossible to copy nature in embroidery-silk. However, another special "behavior" of colors is helpful: colors can influence each other. The effect of a bluish-green is different when used next to blue or to red. The red makes the green greener. Violet is always a mixture of red and blue — if violet is used next to red, it becomes more reddish; next to blue, it becomes more bluish.

When the right color-choice is made, half the work is done.

The second important point to consider is the shading effect colors can give. We all know how colors change, depending on whether viewed by daylight, fluorescent lamps, or other lighting. The same is true of twilight, the darker the surroundings the more colors disappear. As a rule, we will use darker shades of the same color to accentuate the light-shadow effects discussed in "On Symmetry." This was done for example in the designs of Independence Hall (page 23), the Old Boston State House (page 19), and the Carmel Mission (page 41). The basic color in Independence Hall is a reddish-brown. Four shades of the same reddish-brown (DMC 839—842) were used to achieve a realistic shading.

Difficulties arise when an object or building is a white one. In reality, white is rarely untinted by both reflections and "color casts" from surrounding colors, and by the shadows cast by protruding parts of an object. In a design, a "white" building can be shaded with a great many different colors. Although the shading technique is the same, the difference in "emotional feeling" is totally different. Three embroideries can be taken as an example:

1. Mormon Temple, St. George (page 39)
2. D'Evereux, Mississippi (page 29)
3. The Capitol, Washington (page 25)

The first example is shaded with a bluish-grey, giving the building a cool, heavenly, unearthly impression. D'Evereux, Mississippi is much warmer; here a faded rose was used. The Capitol needed many shading colors because of the complex structure. The yellow and grey shades chosen give a more "neutral" impression. Again, a white building is not a totally white building because of the *light*, which gives various degrees of shadow on different parts of the building. Moreover, if subtle differences in shading (colors) were not present, you would see little or no shape at all.

The last example deals with the fact that bright and dark colors can give a "three-dimensional" effect. Used together, bright color surfaces protrude, dark ones give the impression of depth. In scene designs, this can be very important.

After all of the preceeding it must be clear that the proper use of color is very important to the result. When DMC embroidery floss or Paterna persian wool is available, you should have no problems. The DMC numbers are found right on the patterns, and the corresponding numbers for Paterna persian wool are given on page 86—87. If you are working with yarns other than these, the following should be kept in mind: look at the color illustrations and always use the darkest shades where they are used on the originals — if necessary it is better to change the "base" shading color than to mix up the shading. For example: the main color of a building is earth brown, calling for four or five shades of the same brown. The brown in the yarn you happen to be using has only three shades (although this particular yarn does have five shades of red). In this case you would better take five shades of the same red, the darkest red corresponding to the darkest brown, etc., than use, say, the three brown shades plus two red ones.

Another way to solve this problem can be the use of less or more strands of yarn. Using four strands of embroidery floss instead of two will create the effect of one shade darker of a color; one strand instead of two will create the effect of one shade lighter.

As your embroidery will mostly be viewed from a distance, do, from time to time while working, look at it thus. You will see it "growing" — a real creative feeling.

About the Design Illustrations

Cross-stitch has been known for centuries and is still one of the most popular embroidery techniques. It is believed to have originated as a peasant art form in Middle Europe and is very evident in the traditional linen embroidery of the Ukraine and surrounding regions. Americans of the 18th and 19th centuries were especially fond of cross-stitch worked into mottoes and samplers.

The color plates on pages 11—61 show the embroideries in their original sizes. The needlework is mainly cross-stitch and only occasionally is straight stitch used to accentuate shadow lines or lines on towers. Fine evenweave fabric with 30 threads per inch was used for the models.

Color indications for all designs are given according to the color-chart of DMC six-strand mouliné special embroidery floss. On this fabric two strands were used. In some designs, occasionally one strand was used. This is indicated beside the number with a ', e.g. 501'.

When using coarser linen, the thickness should be increased, in which case it is preferable to use three strands for two threads of material and two strands for the numbers indicated with '.

On pages 86—87, the DMC numbers are "translated" into the numbers of the Paterna persian yarn color-chart.

On these pages you can also find which colors are used in each design. This will allow you to make a second or third embroidery, according to the leftover material.

Each square on the pattern represents two threads of the fabric and one cross-stitch. The cross-stitch technique will be discussed on pages 78—79.

Each symbol on the pattern represents the color-number beside the scheme on the pattern. The patterns all have their own color scheme.

With the exception of the borders, diagrams corresponding to color plates appear in sequence on pages 90–111.

Fabric

Easy to master, cross-stitch can be worked on a variety of fabrics.

Any *evenweave* fabric (having the same number of threads per inch in each direction of the fabric) is suitable for cross-stitch and the best fabrics for the purpose are those whose threads can be easily seen and counted.

EVENWEAVE FABRICS

In evenweave fabrics, the horizontal and vertical threads are woven the same distance apart, so the same number of threads in each direction will form a perfect square. This enables the making of a perfectly square stitch into the openings formed by the intersections of the horizontal and vertical threads of the fabric.

Three basic types of evenweave fabric most commonly used for cross-stitch are EVENWEAVE LINEN, HARDANGER, and AIDA CLOTH.

EVENWEAVE LINEN is a finely woven material in which threads are counted for the placement of stitches. Since linen is often woven with a thick thread alternating with a thin thread, stitches are taken over two threads in order to make even stitches. Linen is most commonly available in white, off-white, and cream colors. Before working with linen fabric it would be advisable to have some experience working on aida cloth, because of the three fabrics most widely used, aida cloth most clearly indicates where the stitches should be placed.

In HARDANGER, a cotton cloth somewhat coarser than linen, each horizontal and vertical intersection is formed by pairs of threads worked over and under each other, providing an easily discernable separation at each intersection for the placing of stitches.

AIDA CLOTH is a basketweave cotton fabric whose horizontal and vertical divisions consist of many strands of interlocking threads worked over and under together, forming definite openings clearly showing where to stitch. Aida is usually available in a wide range of colors.

Both hardanger and aida cloth are usually worked over one square of the fabric.

To aid in cross-stitching on fabrics whose threads cannot be easily seen and counted, a special embroidery canvas called Blue Line canvas can be used. The Blue Line canvas is basted to the fabric and the yarn is worked carefully over it into the fabric below; when the cross-stitching is completed, the special canvas is removed thread by thread. Only then are any straight stitches made. This special canvas can also be used for cross-stitching on fabrics that are not evenweave. (In this case bear in mind that it is the size of the Blue Line canvas, not the size or weave of the material underneath it, that will determine the exact size of your finished color design.)

NEEDLEPOINT CANVAS can also be used for cross-stitch. This will result in a larger finished piece as needlepoint canvas is a coarser or more open fabric than evenweave linen, hardanger, or aida cloth. For canvas three-ply persian wool or six (or more) ply embroidery floss is usually used, and as with linen, stitches are taken over two canvas threads. When working on canvas, the background should be worked in a suitable (preferably bright) neutral color. This background will always represent the sky. Start the background ten to fifteen crosses on top of the design. A tower needs less space on top than a "scenery."

The diagrams in this book can be used to execute the designs in standard needlepoint stitches such as continental (tent) or basketweave (diagonal tent) stitch — but especially in such design elements as buildings you will not be able to achieve a true representation (cross-stitches are in effect little squares or blocks whereas the needlepoint stitches mentioned are all worked in the same direction, resulting in more "jagged" edges).

Yarn

Cross-stitch can be worked in a wide variety of yarns (embroidery floss, "pearl cotton," linen, silk, crewel yarn, persian wool, tapestry wool, even worsted knitting yarns), according to the fabric you are working on, the texture and scale you wish to achieve, and your personal taste (and pocketbook). The diagrams in this book have been keyed to two specific types of yarn because they offer a very wide range of colors, are sturdy, and are commonly available in American art needlework stores and centers.

DMC embroidery floss ("six-strand mouliné special") is a 6-ply cotton yarn. It can be split and used in any number of ply. Due to its silky luster it (and "pearl cotton") are often referred to as "silk."

Paternayan persian wool is a 3-ply 100% virgin wool yarn. Depending upon the fabric or gauge of needlepoint canvas chosen, it can be split and used in 1, 2, or 3-ply.

There is a difference in the thickness and ply of yarn. Persian wool, for example, is 3-ply and cotton floss is typically 6-ply. However, 3-ply wool is thicker than 6-ply cotton. Some people work with a looser tension than others and may want to use a strand less yarn than those who work with very tight tension. Those who work with tight stitches may want to use a strand or two more. To see what is best for your way of working, experiment with various thicknesses of yarn in the margin of your planned piece or on a fabric scrap.

From Graph to Fabric

The size of the finished cross-stitch is determined by the fabric selected. The size of the finished design will not necessarily correspond with the size of the graph unless the actual number of threads to the inch is the same as the squares to the inch on the graph. This will be determined by the number of threads or stitches per inch of the fabric you are using. Each square on the graph represents one square or one complete cross-stitch on the fabric.

The best way to ascertain how many stitches can be made on your fabric is to hold a ruler alongside a vertical or horizontal thread of the fabric and count the number of threads to the inch. An aid to doing this is to touch each thread as you count with the point of your needle. Since stitching on evenweave linen requires covering two threads in each direction, divide the total number of threads in half to get the number of stitches per inch on the fabric. Then count the number of squares on the graph of your pattern. Add enough fabric to provide a margin all around, or a border design plus a margin, and at least an extra inch all around for use in mounting or finishing. In addition, the size of the fabric should be large enough to accommodate your hoop (if you will be using one) from the outer edge of the design.

To change the size of your design, simply use a fabric with more or less threads to the inch. That is, the looser the weave of the fabric, the larger the design will be. It is also possible to enlarge a design by having your stitch cover more than one thread. If you stitch over two squares each way instead of one for hardanger, and four threads instead of two for evenweave linen, you will increase the size of your stitch four times. Take care, however, not to cover too many threads of fabric as this may cause slacking in your embroidery yarn. It is useful to experiment on a scrap of fabric first. To enlarge a design on aida cloth, it is recommended that you use an aida cloth with fewer squares to the inch.

General Materials

The materials needed for cross-stitchery are: a piece of evenweave fabric, an embroidery hoop if you are accustomed to using one, a tapestry needle, a thimble (optional), a pair of embroidery or other sharp scissors, and embroidery yarn.

It is advisable to use a hoop to maintain even tension and

avoid distorting the fabric. The hoop will also keep the fabric taut, making the holes easier to see. Use a small wood or plastic hoop with a screw-type tension adjuster. When working on needlepoint canvas you may wish to use a frame to maintain even tension.

Though I do not use a hoop, to save back and eyes I always use a little cushion on which my embroidery lays flat; it is closer to my eyes, and does not crease. Really worth a try.

The tapestry needle should be blunt rather than sharp since you are working through an existing opening in the fabric, not making one. Never leave the needle piercing the fabric between uses. The needle may snag the fabric or it may tarnish and stain the fabric. If you do not use a needlecase, keep your needle only in the margin area of the fabric.

Bear in mind that you may wish to use more than one needle at the same time. I always work with at least ten needles, each one being ready for use in a certain color.

In cross-stitch, as in all forms of embroidery, you should be using the "stab" technique. This means that the stitch is done with two motions — i.e., push in, pull down, push up, pull out, etc. — rather than a single in-and-out "scooping" or sewing stitch. The "scooping" method has a tendency to pull most forms of embroidery out of shape and you will find that the "stabbing" method will keep your tension even and your stitches neater.

Always remove a hoop when not in use. This will keep your fabric from developing a permanent ridge from the hoop. Placing the hoop over an existing stitch will not affect it, however, a little "fluffing" with a needle may be necessary if the hoop has flattened the stitch.

Keep a pair of embroidery scissors handy and do not use them for any other purpose. If you have to remove stitches, use your small, pointed embroidery scissors to snip them carefully. If you try to go back the other way to remove a stitch, you may tangle or weaken the yarn.

A magnifying glass hanging from a cord or chain around your neck is an excellent aid for close work.

Stitch Diagrams

The Cross-Stitch and the Straight Stitch will both work nicely on needlepoint canvas as well as evenweave linen, hardanger, etc. Remember that the relationship between the graph and the finished piece will vary according to the fabric used. Both stitches are used in needlepoint so you will not have any trouble adapting them to canvas. When using canvas for cross-stitch, a 12-gauge canvas is recommended. Aida cloth looks like a cross between evenweave linen and needlepoint canvas. To avoid confusion, a separate set of stitch diagrams for aida cloth have been included.

CROSS-STITCH TECHNIQUE

There are two ways of making the Cross-Stitch. (A) Completing each cross as you work or (B) Executing half the cross as you work across the fabric and completing the other half as you work back.

In the following diagrams the fabric is represented "schematically" rather than "three-dimensionally," to make the diagrams simpler to "read" and follow.

STRAIGHT STITCH

To supplement the Cross-Stitch you will also need the Straight Stitch. It is only an accent stitch for use where the Cross-Stitch is too large for the desired effect. Straight stitches must always be made after finishing the Cross-stitches.

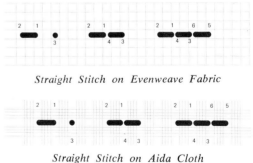

Straight Stitch on Evenweave Fabric

Straight Stitch on Aida Cloth

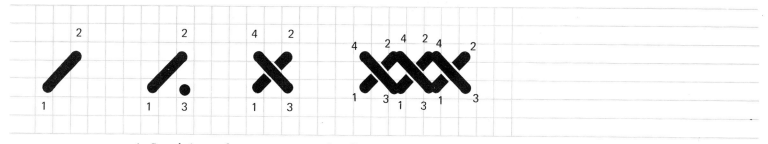

A. Completing each cross as you work will give you heavier coverage and make the cross more visible.

B. Working the cross in two journeys across the fabric will take less time to cover an area.
Working from left to right, lay the first half of the cross. When you have finished, start a return journey to complete the cross.

CROSS-STITCH ON AIDA CLOTH

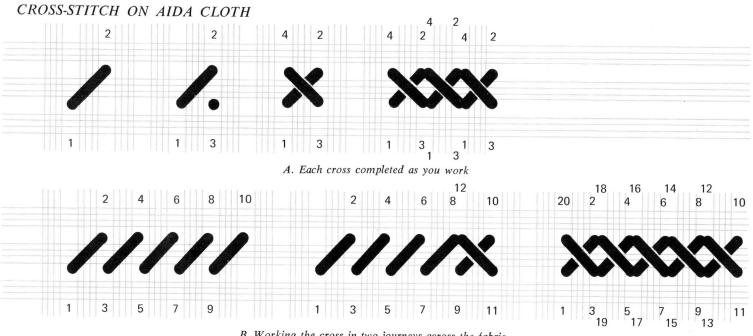

A. Each cross completed as you work

B. Working the cross in two journeys across the fabric

General Technique

It is important that the selvage (edge of a woven fabric finished off to keep from ravelling) of your fabric be to the right or left of your design, never at the top or bottom. If the piece of fabric you buy is a small cut from a large bolt, no selvage may be indicated. You can determine the side of the selvage by pulling a thread in each direction. The horizontal thread will be "crinklier" than the vertical thread. The cut edges of the fabric should be bound by:

Basting the edges under or whip-stitching over, or;
Making zigzag stitches on the edges, or;
Stitching double-fold bias tape over the edges.

It is best to start stitching from the center of the design. You can find the center by gently folding the fabric in half and basting along the fold. Unfold the fabric and fold it in half again in the opposite direction, making another row of basting stitches. The center of the fabric is the point where the basted stitches cross. If the exact center of the design is not a comfortable place to start (it might be an unstitched portion of the background), begin somewhere off center. However, find that place by counting from the center of the graph to the place where you intend to start, then counting from the center to the corresponding place on your fabric.

If possible work the darkest colors first — vertical or horizontal lines, roads, shadow-stripes on buildings, windows. Some parts of the designs are just filled in with one color — look at the color picture, if there are no little objects in the "field" you can work straight on without counting!

Leave, if possible, the white parts for the very last moment. Even if you work quickly, white very soon becomes dingy and smudgy.

Leave about one inch of yarn on the back of the fabric, holding it in position with your forefinger. When you work your first stitches, work them over this tail of yarn on the back to secure it. This is done instead of making knots in

embroidery, avoiding lumps when the piece is finished and framed or mounted.

If possible, plan as much of the route of your embroidery, especially color changes, so that the reverse side is as neat as possible. Never leave long, loose yarn on the reverse side and never carry long strands of yarn from place to place on the front of existing work. Try to weave under existing stitches or finish off and begin again.

When you finish off one color, run your needle under and over the stitches of the last row on the back of the piece, being careful not to pull too tightly. For extra security, make a loop over the last stitch on the back of the fabric and cut the yarn as close as possible without leaving a tail.

It is preferable to make straight stitches after completing the cross-stitches. Straight stitches allow for movement in the designs unobtainable with the cross-stitch, and are used to form lines where necessary and to accentuate shadow lines.

Each symbol on the graph corresponds to a certain color. Since the graph is in black and white, you can make your own color chart (to avoid confusing the shades) for each design by noting the symbol on a card and pulling that color yarn through the card next to the symbol. You can arrange all your working yarn in this fashion on a large piece of thin cardboard by making holes about three-quarters of an inch away from the edge to accommodate all your colors, and fastening the yarn in a slipknot in the hole next to the appropriate symbol. If you wish to have a chart that does not have to be made up separately for each design, note the color *number,* rather than symbol, next to each color of yarn on your card.

Borders

The border motifs on pages 55-61 can be repeated as often as desired. The geometric motifs can be worked in any color combinations. Changing the colors in the Indian borders is possible, too, but the "Indian" outlook may need at least the turquoise or reddish-brown shades.

Borders can be used on tablecloths, cushions, place mats, curtains, clothing (see also the general "Uses" suggestions on p. 83.) Borders can be worked on all kinds of fabric. If you wish to use fabric that is not evenweave, this is possible, too, with the use of the special canvas discussed on page 76.

The smaller borders can be used to frame the scenery designs in this book. Try, in that case, to use colors that appear in the scene, taking care the border is not too dominant. The border should add something, not spoil or overwhelm the scene. Before you start you might try putting loose threads of the desired colors around the picture, to help decide if the choice is a good one.

When working with color combinations remember to start with the darkest colors first; darker colors are usually the detail in a design and are always completed first. Leaving the lighter colors to be worked last will also keep your work cleaner.

When working a square piece, measure the size you want the finished piece to be. The border pattern should be a perfect square fitting the dimensions of your finished piece. The interior design, or scenery, should be centered, both side to side and top to bottom, as if the border is a frame. The dimensions of the border should be marked on the cloth or canvas for easy reference with a straight or safety pin. After you center the border motif (the center of the "basic repeat unit" of the design you have chosen should be lined up with the exact center of each of the border sides) it will be easier to work from the center out to the corners. This will enable you to plan the meeting of the four corners. Typically, the border repeat units will either work out perfectly to the corner, or end a little short or a little long of a perfect repeat of the basic repeat pattern. If so, you must determine for yourself how you want the corners to look, and either use your ingenuity to "miter" the corners in an attractive way (the corners shown on pages 59 and 61 are a good example of this), do the corners in a solid color, or center a portion of the border design in each corner. (This is a good reason for working from the center to the corners — "irregularities" of design are less obtrusive, and coped with more easily, at the corners.)

When working a rectangular piece, the procedure is exactly the same. In either case it is important to center your motif precisely, for when you reach a corner, your motif may end irregularly and the opposite side must end on the same irregularity to balance the look of your border.

The corners on the patterns will make it possible to work closed borders. In this case you must keep in mind that a longer "repeat pattern" (such as the fish border) needs more planning. (In general, the longer a border pattern is before it repeats the more likely the finished piece will be larger than you originally had in mind. As a rule this is no problem as "long-repeat" borders are mostly used for items such as tablecloths.)

Alphabets and Numbers

Letters and numbers can be embroidered in any color that you like. The patterns of the large letters show that two colors are used.

It could be fun to embroider a cushion with your favorite scenery on the front, and for instance the word LOVE, embroidered with large letters on the back. Each letter could be in a different color!

The combination of letters, numbers, sayings, mottoes, scenes, borders, etc., will make creative and colorful samplers.

The smaller numbers and letters are the ideal size to add an interesting touch to your other needlepoints by working your initials and date of completion at the bottom of the work.

Letters can be used as borders by working the title or information about the subject matter instead of a border design. For more detail about the subject matter, work a two-sided pillow or cushion with the scene on one side and the information on the other.

When working with alphabets and numbers:

Select the appropriate size, i.e., small, medium, large, for the piece you wish to make.

Count the number of letters in the word or words you intend to use. IMPORTANT: Don't forget to count the spaces between each word when using more than one.

With a ruler, measure the length of the word or words and the height of the letters.

Center this measurement top to bottom and side to side on the piece of cloth or canvas you are using.

Begin to work the letters from left to right — the same direction as if you were writing them.

The process for working the three sets of numbers (see illustration) is the same as indicated above.

Ironing

Place your finished work, face down, on a clean piece of terry cloth on your ironing board. Place another piece of clean terry cloth over the work and iron with a medium steam setting. Ironing on terry cloth enables the stitches to "breathe" and they are not flattened by the action of the iron. Do not iron your work if you have used needlepoint canvas and persian wool. The wool will flatten if ironed. Instead, block a needlepoint cross-stitch piece as you would any other piece of needlepoint. Using stainless-steel pushpins, tack the piece, face up, to a board and into its original shape. Dampen (do not *soak* the fabric under any circumstances!) with water from a spray bottle or plant mister and leave to dry. Repeat the process until it has been blocked back to its original shape.

Mounting and Framing

Unless you are an expert seamstress and have experience in finishing and framing, take your finished piece to an upholsterer or needlework shop to be mounted onto a cushion, chair seat, pillow, etc., or mounted for a hanging or framed work. Your local framer or finisher will have a variety of molding or fabric backings to choose from. Glass is not recommended as it flattens the stitches and the texture of the work is lost.

Before having your embroidery framed, carefully cut off any threads at the backside. Especially if worked on fine fabric, loose threads on the back will be visible on the right side, spoiling the final view.

Suggestions for Use of Cross-Stitch Scenes and Borders

Purse
Tote bag
Cosmetic case
Eyeglass case
Desk set
Belt
Cummerbund
Vest
Suspenders
Shawl
Hair band
Hat band
Hostess apron
Collars, cuffs, and other clothing trimmings

For the House:

Wall hangings
Samplers
Picture frames
Window valance
Window shades
Lamp base
Tray table
Footstool
Pillows
Chair cushion
Tablecloth
Bedspread
Rug
Wastebasket
Captain's or director's chair
Luggage rack straps
Book cover
Doorstop (brick cover)

Bell pull
Tea cozy
Toaster (or other appliance) cover
Coasters
Glassed place mats

For small or narrow pieces you can "zero in" on a part or detail of a scene or design (for example, for a set of coasters you could break out your favorite states from the color map of the U.S.).

For a large wall hanging (or a rug) six or eight scenes could be pieced together in a "travelogue" running down or across.

Suppliers of Cross-Stitch Materials

The following will take mail orders for cross-stitch materials (or direct you to a shop handling them in your locality). You should contact them before submitting an order to determine their terms and shipping arrangements.

My Favorite Things, Inc.
6129 Far Hills Avenue
Dayton, Ohio 45459

Scandinavian Shop
134 Main
Dike, Iowa 50624

Merribee Needlecraft
2904 West Lancaster
Fort Worth, Texas 76107

Needlecraft Shop
4501 Van Nuys Boulevard
Sherman Oaks, California 91403

Thumbelina
1685 Copenhagen Drive
Solvang, California 93463

Gina Brown Needlecrafts Studio
1230A 17th Avenue S.W.
Calgary, Alberta T2T 0B8

The Needlepoint Shop
Route 44A, Bolton Notch
Box 516, Bolton, Connecticut 06040

The Lightning Splitter
RR1, Box 225
Bernardston, Massachusetts 01337

American Crewel and Canvas Studio
P.O. Box 298
Boonton, New Jersey 07005

Judy's Originals
182 Mt. Bethel Road
Warren, New Jersey 07060

Wallis Mayers Needlework, Inc.
780 Madison Avenue
New York, N.Y. 10021

Boutique Margot
26 West 54th Street
New York, N.Y. 10019

Paternayan Bros., Inc.
312 E. 95th Street
New York, N.Y. 10028

Stitchcraft
4 Station Plaza
Glen Head, N.Y. 11545

Ball of Yarn
1208 Gordon Street
Charlotte, North Carolina 28205

Ginnie Thompson Originals
P.O. Box 825
Pawley's Island, South Carolina 29585

Heirloom Art Needlework
5256 Memorial Drive
Stone Mountain, Georgia 30085

Needlearts, Inc.
2211 Monroe
Dearborn, Michigan 48124

Color Chart

PATERNA WOOL → / DMC SILK ↓	334	262	285	182	186	528	532	612	R74	266	274	530	436	249	180	184	186	462	144	154	172	174	194	133	143	153	510	555	570	575	522	546	556	765	760	114	124	134	136	217	020	162	164	166	168	441	437	521	531	479	454	271	455	015	396
(DMC SILK)	311	315	316	317	318	319	320	327	347	355	356	367	402	407	413	414	415	420	433	434	435	436	437	451	452	453	469	470	471	472	501	502	503	519	597	610	611	612	613	632	644	645	646	647	648	725	727	731	733	734	738	739	745	746	747
MAP U.S.											•	•						•					•					•	•	•	•	•	•				•	•										•								•
EVERYVILLAGE, VERMONT						•				•		•		•	•	•		•			•								•				•				•	•	•			•						•	•						
PORTSMOUTH			•			•						•			•	•													•							•	•	•		•		•					•								
MYSTIC SEAPORT						•			•														•													•	•	•		•	•		•												
OLD BOSTON STATE HOUSE														•	•	•							•														•		•		•	•		•											
MOUNT VERNON							•				•			•	•												•		•												•	•										•			
INDEPENDENCE HALL				•										•	•																						•		•			•		•									•		
U.S. CAPITOL				•							•	•		•	•												•					•						•		•	•	•	•	•		•	•		•						
COLONIAL WILLIAMSBURG			•	•		•									•									•	•		•	•		•																•		•						•	
D'EVEREUX		•				•					•			•	•	•	•		•					•	•		•			•	•					•						•						•						•	
FRENCH QUARTER	•			•	•										•					•				•	•	•	•										•		•			•	•		•		•				•	•			•
FARM IN HILL COUNTRY						•	•				•	•		•	•	•													•		•	•	•		•							•		•							•				
"AMERICAN PATCHWORK"						•	•				•	•				•												•	•	•	•														•								•		
HIGH LAKE		•		•		•																	•			•			•			•		•					•																
ST. GEORGE TEMPLE											•	•																•		•												•					•				•				
CARMEL MISSION	•		•	•		•	•		•		•	•		•	•	•		•							•		•	•	•	•												•						•		•		•		•	•
SANTA BARBARA						•	•				•	•								•					•			•										•	•		•			•	•		•					•	•	•		
SAN FRANCISCO				•		•	•		•		•												•					•		•							•		•			•								•					
NEW YORK				•										•	•	•		•						•	•											•	•					•			•								•	•	
LAS VEGAS								•	•				•					•			•	•	•											•			•	•								•		•						•	•
SOUTHWEST DESERTS			•			•	•		•	•															•												•	•		•			•	•		•		•						•	•
FLOWER BORDER	•							•		•				•															•	•	•																			•					
FISH BORDER	•									•	•		•	•		•					•																•	•		•			•									•	•			
GEOMETRIC BORDER										•																									•																				•
INDIAN BORDER	•										•																								•																		•	•	

Conversion chart — PATERNA WOOL (top number) / DMC SILK (bottom number)

Location	312/797	741/799	104/801	211/814	365/823	395/827	531/833	112/838	116/839	126/840	132/841	138/842	108/844	145/869	516/890	G64/906	G74/907	414/920	416/922	346/924	389/926	391/927	392/928	380/930	381/931	506/934	504/936	505/937	257/950	288/962	Y44/973	405/975	G30/992	G32/993	540/3011	553/3012	590/3013	110/3021	573/3022	563/3023	513/3024	837/3033	615/3041	137/3042	466/3045	541/3046	492/3047	512/3051	594/3052	032/3072	232/3350	250/3687	256/3689	014/ECRU	026/WHITE
MAP U.S.									•				•	•				•	•						•									•					•							•	•	•							•
EVERYVILLAGE, VERMONT													•								•			•	•	•		•										•	•							•	•	•						•	•
PORTSMOUTH									•		•	•	•								•	•		•												•	•	•	•	•						•	•	•	•					•	•
MYSTIC SEAPORT									•	•	•	•	•								•	•	•			•										•		•	•		•					•	•							•	•
OLD BOSTON STATE HOUSE			•		•	•						•			•						•	•	•															•	•	•							•							•	•
MOUNT VERNON									•	•	•	•	•	•	•						•	•				•									•		•		•		•					•	•							•	•
INDEPENDENCE HALL										•	•	•	•									•						•									•							•	•									•	•
U.S. CAPITOL					•						•	•								•	•				•	•									•			•						•				•	•					•	•
COLONIAL WILLIAMSBURG									•	•	•	•										•						•									•									•	•			•			•	•
D'EVEREUX										•		•									•		•			•	•	•					•		•	•		•								•	•	•	•			•	•
FRENCH QUARTER									•	•	•	•		•			•					•			•		•	•							•	•	•	•		•	•		•				•				•			•	•
FARM IN HILL COUNTRY									•	•	•	•	•								•	•				•		•					•	•							•					•							•	•
"AMERICAN PATCHWORK"												•		•	•	•																										•					•	•							
HIGH LAKE										•			•								•	•						•					•	•	•			•				•				•	•	•					•	•
ST. GEORGE TEMPLE									•				•								•	•	•	•		•		•														•		•										•
CARMEL MISSION		•							•			•	•		•									•									•					•				•		•	•		•	•						•
SANTA BARBARA									•												•	•	•		•		•											•				•		•		•			•			•	•
SAN FRANCISCO											•		•								•		•			•		•									•		•	•					•	•								•
NEW YORK									•	•	•	•	•								•		•			•		•						•				•	•	•	•					•							•	•
LAS VEGAS	•	•	•		•				•	•	•	•	•				•													•	•	•	•		•				•																•
SOUTHWEST DESERTS												•														•	•	•							•	•			•			•						•		•				•
FLOWER BORDER	•											•													•		•																			•	•							
FISH BORDER						•						•													•	•																				•	•							
GEOMETRIC BORDER							•															•						•											•							•									•
INDIAN BORDER												•					•																•						•					•											

Working Diagrams

Be sure to read Instructions carefully.

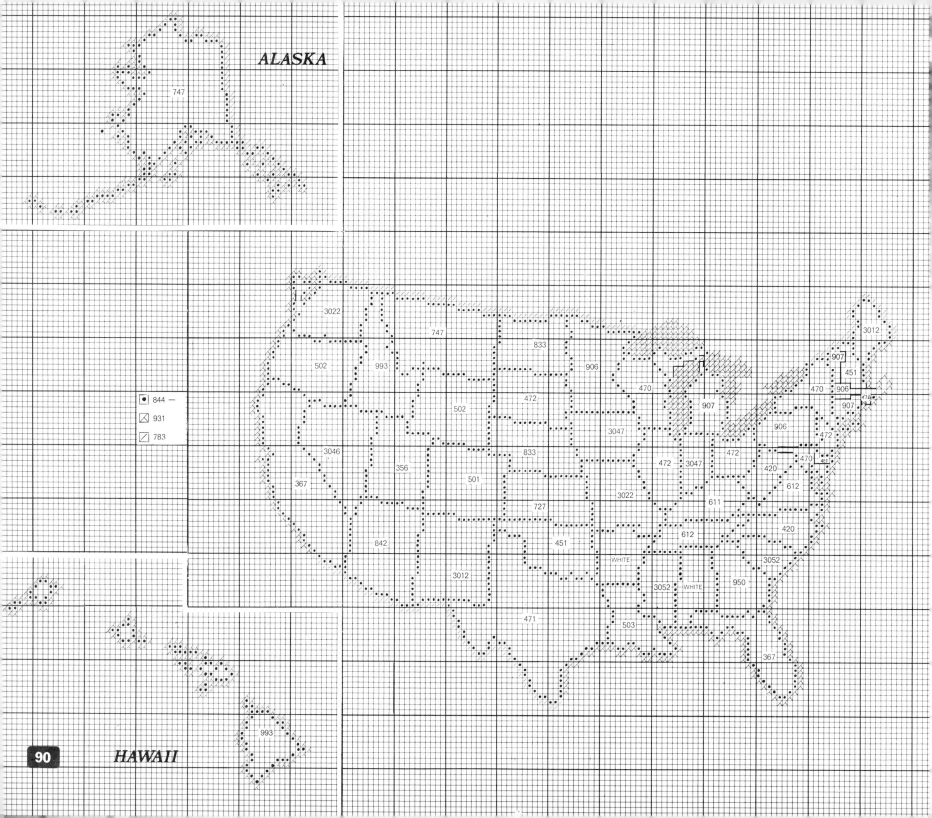

ALASKA

747

502 993

3022

747

833

906 3012

502

472

470 907 451

3047 470 906

907 470

3046

367 356 501

833

3022

727

842

451

3012

3052 WHITE

471 503

• 844 —

☒ 931

◪ 783

906

472

472 3047 420

612

611 612 420

3052

950

367

HAWAII

993

⬣	319	☝	355	⊞	3046
☒	3051	⊙	733	⊡	WHITE
◪	471	Ⓝ	407	◪	415
⊟	420	☐	367	⊟	ECRU
⊟	3013	▲	930	◨	413
■	844	⋀	435	◨	934
⊠	646	▨	783	◩	731
⊢	502	⊟	611	V	613
‖	931	◪	3021	Y	937
◺	3047	◢	632		
▯	414	Y	926		

91

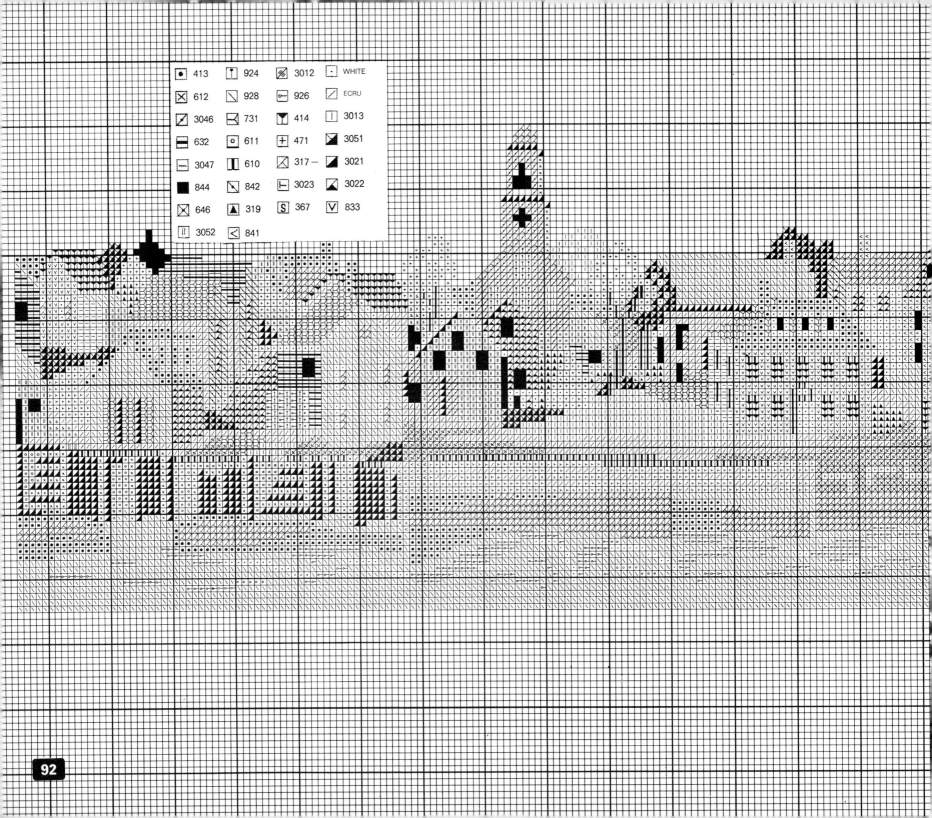

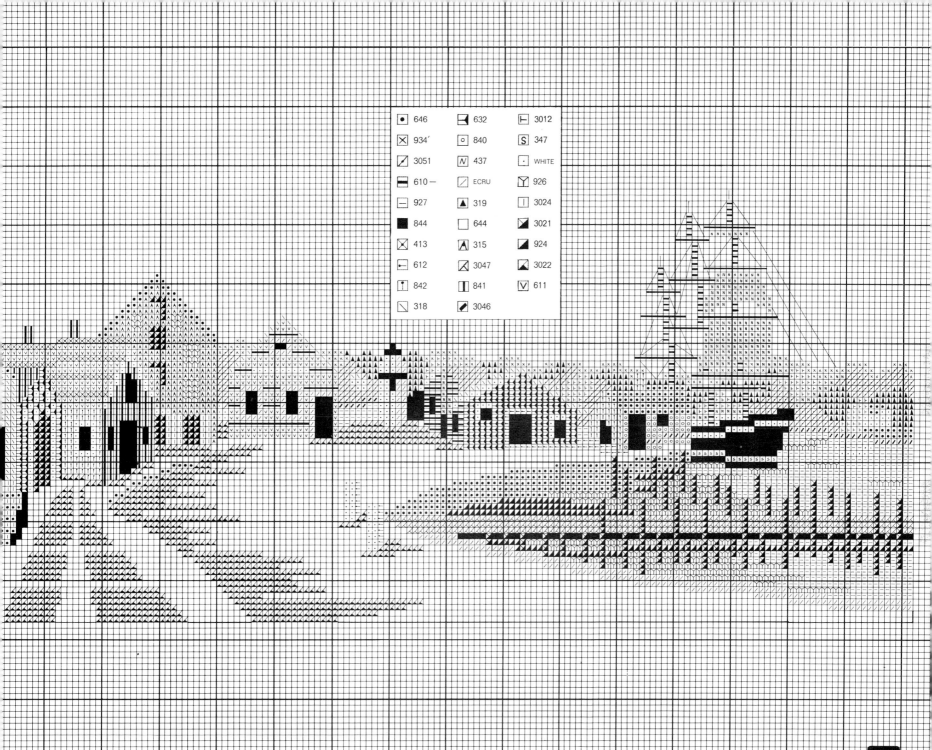

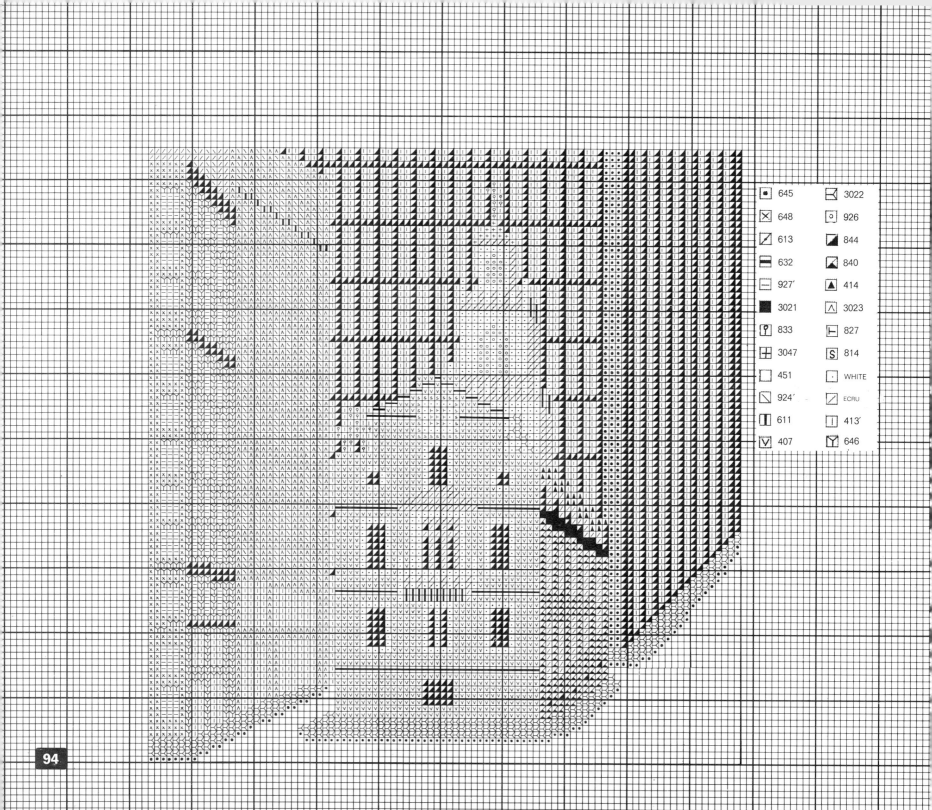

•	645		3022
⊠	648	⊙	926
⊘	613	◤	844
⊟	632	◣	840
⊟	927´	▲	414
■	3021	∧	3023
⚲	833	⊢	827
⊞	3047	S	814
▯	451	·	WHITE
◩	924´	⊘	ECRU
◫	611	I	413´
⋁	407	Y	646

317
841
648
611 —
739
3021
869
3045
927
840
950
839 —
407
WHITE
ECRU —
632
842
413 —
646
3046
613

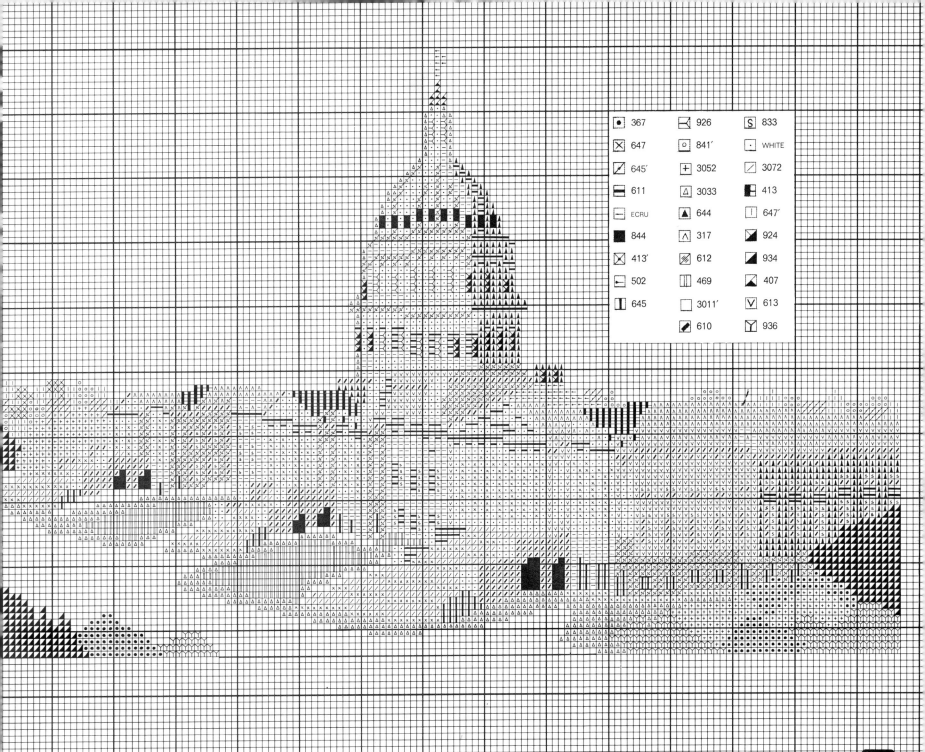

•	367	⊟	926	S	833
✕	647	⊡	841′	·	WHITE
⧄	645′	⊞	3052	⧄	3072
⊟	611	△	3033	◨	413
⊟	ECRU	▲	644	‖	647′
■	844	⋀	317	◹	924
⊠	413′	▨	612	◢	934
⊢	502	‖	469	◣	407
‖	645	☐	3011′	V	613
◢	610	⊻	936		

97

⊡ 317	Ɪ 3021	◸ 841
⊠ 3046	⊙ 840	◹ 745
◿ 648	☐ 613	Ɪ ECRU
▬ 839 〰	▼ 451	◪ 645
⊟ 472	⊞ 927	◥ 319
■ 413 〰	⋀ 3052	◣ 469
⊠ 3051	◢ 937	⊽ 470
⊢ 842	◥ 924	⊻ 452
Ⓢ 3687	⋅ WHITE	

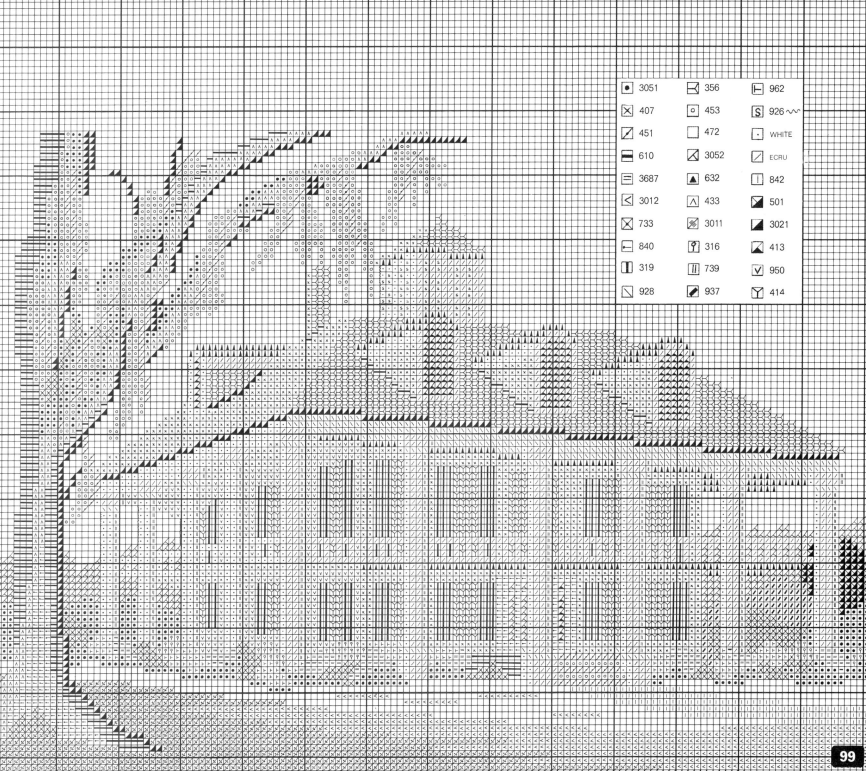

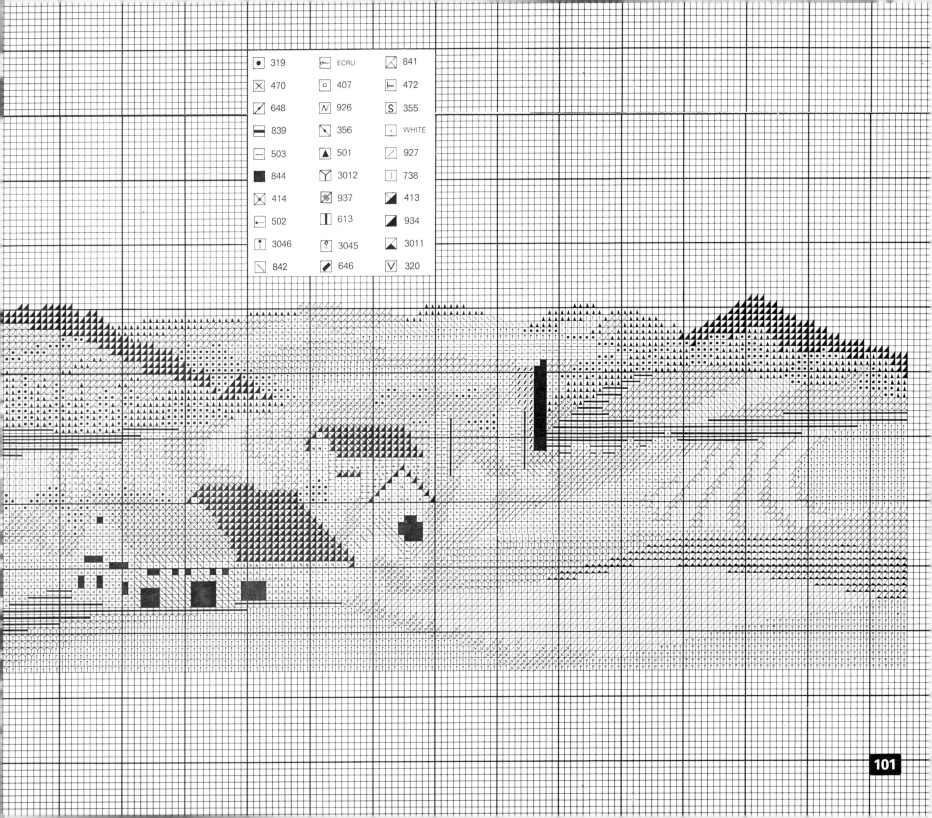

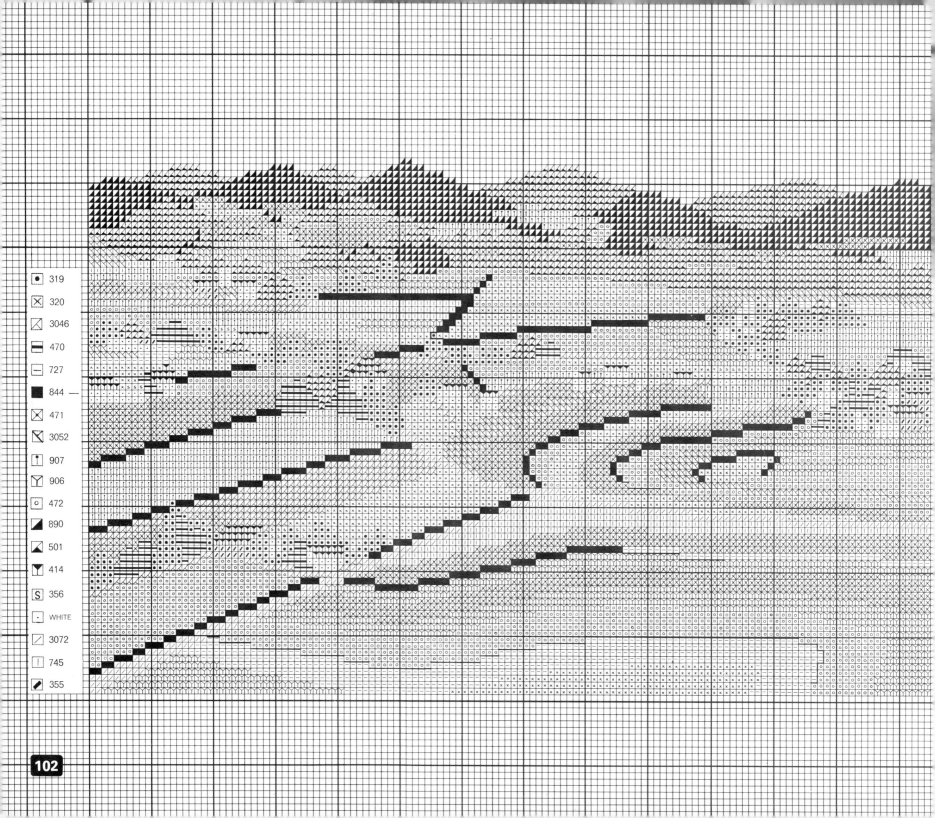

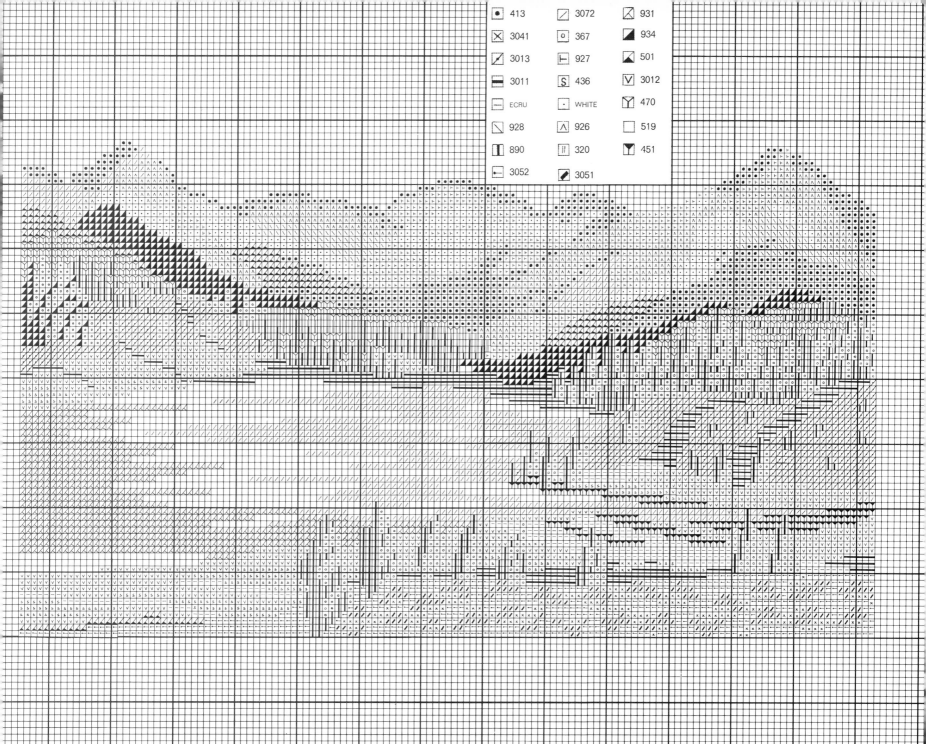

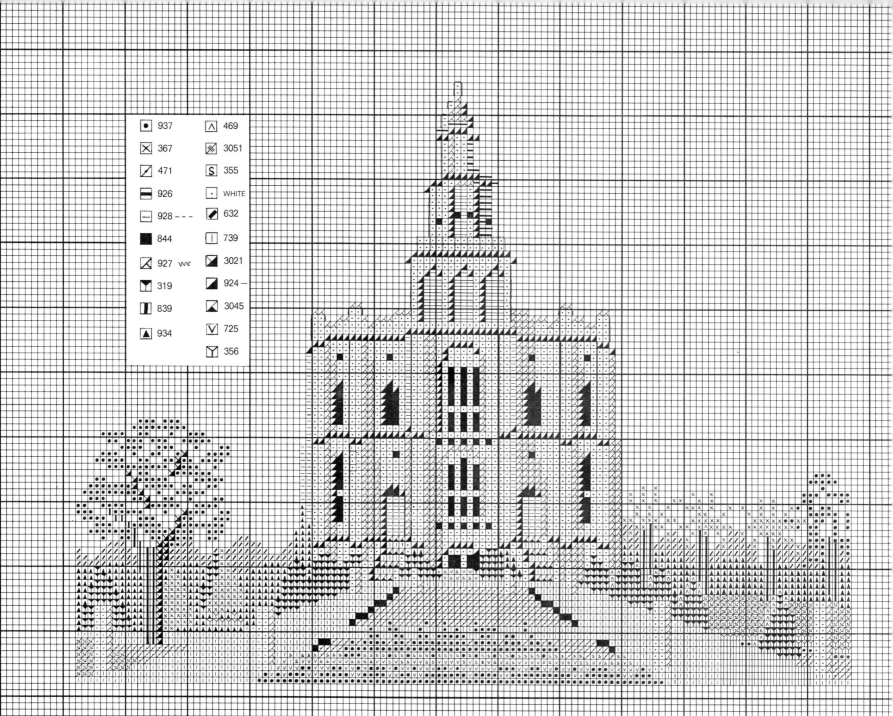

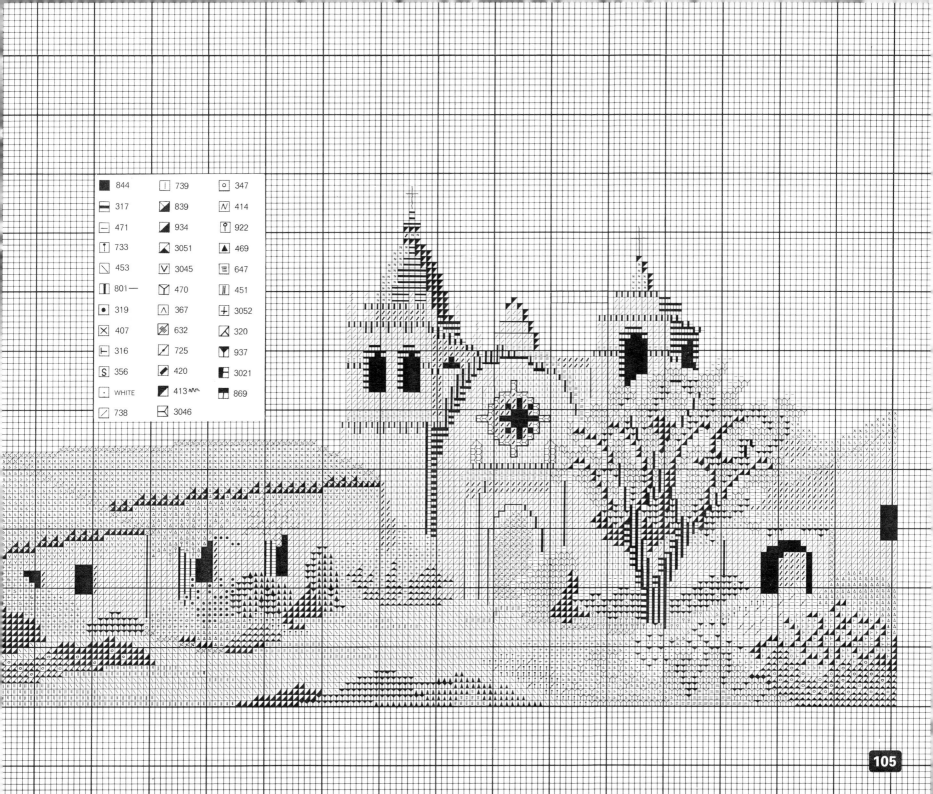

■	844	⊓	739	⊙	347
⊟	317	◩	839	Ɲ	414
⊡	471	◪	934	⅋	922
⥮	733	◸	3051	▲	469
⟍	453	⩔	3045	≣	647
⊓	801—	�⅄	470	‖	451
⊙	319	⋀	367	⊞	3052
⊠	407	▨	632	⧄	320
⊢	316	⟋	725	⅄	937
S	356	◹	420	⊨	3021
·	WHITE	◿	413 ⌁	⊩	869
⟋	738	⊠	3046		

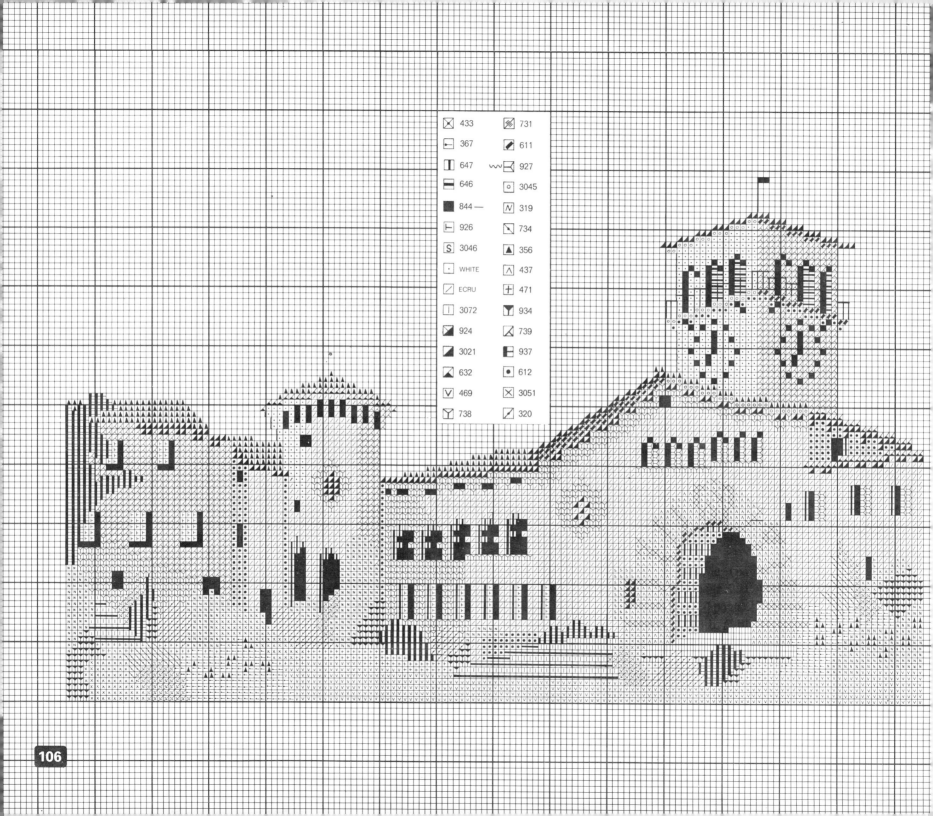

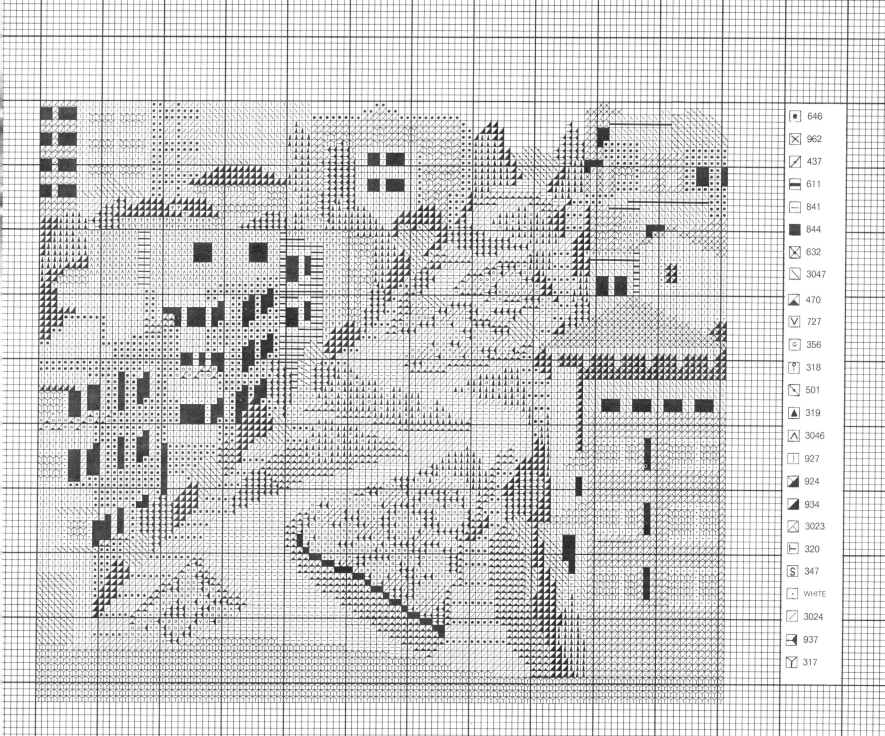

◉	646	
⊠	962	
⟋	437	
⊟	611	
⊟	841	
■	844	
⊠	632	
◺	3047	
◪	470	
V	727	
◎	356	
⌧	318	
◩	501	
▲	319	
⋀	3046	
⊞	927	
◪	924	
◢	934	
⊠	3023	
⊢	320	
S	347	
⊡	WHITE	
⧄	3024	
◳	937	
Y	317	

107

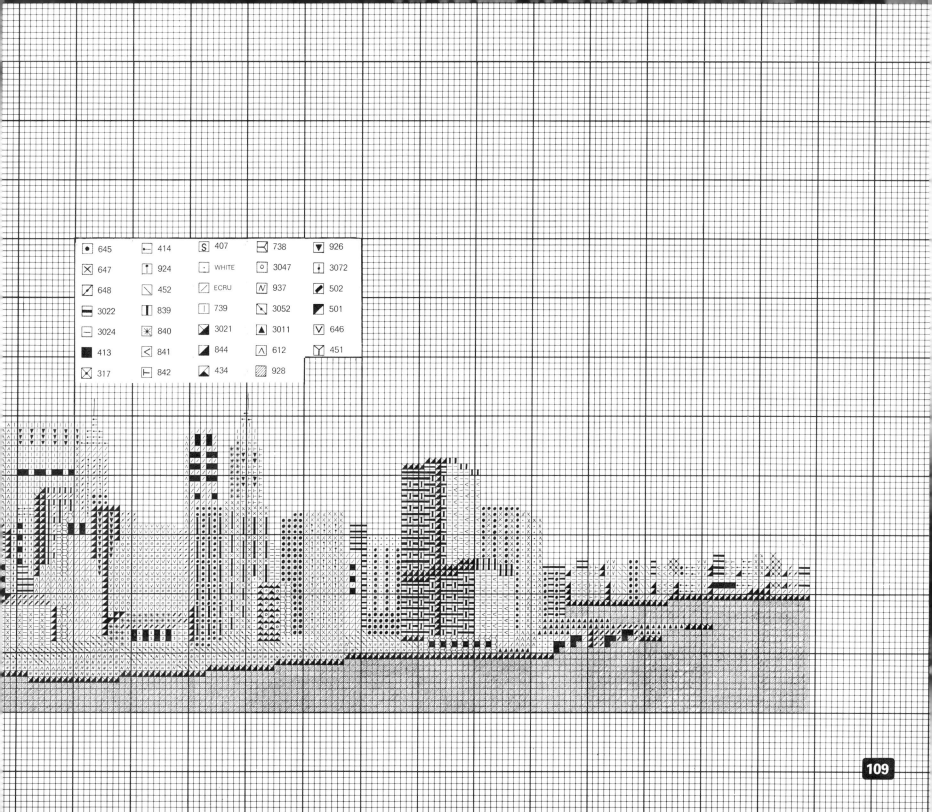

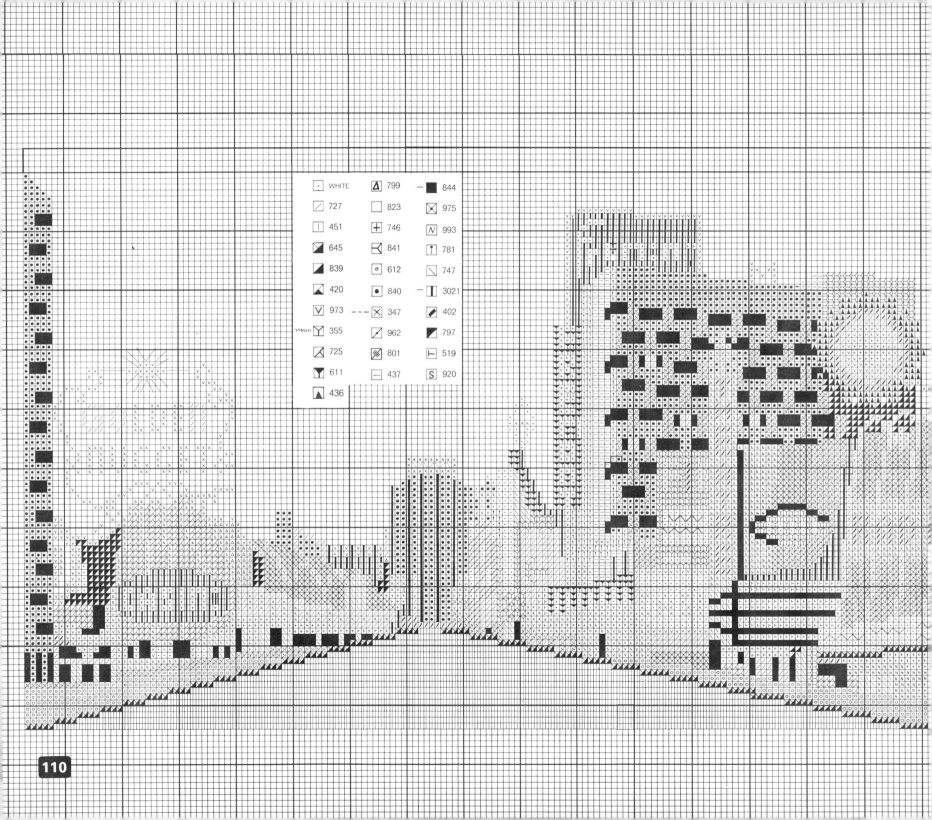

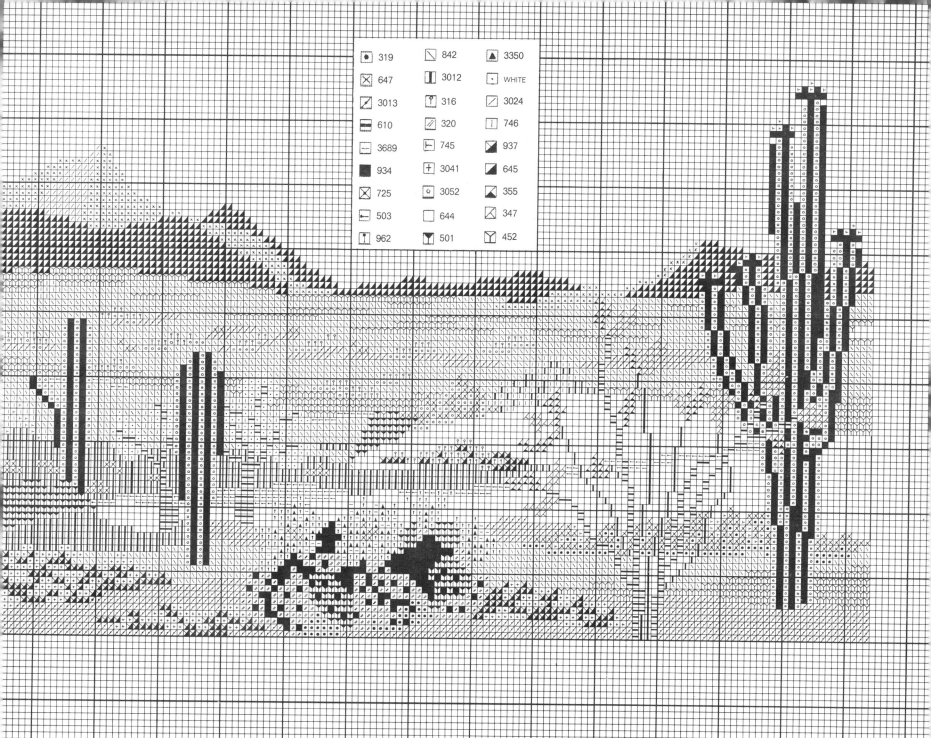